40 Day
TRUE SELF
Devotional

40 Days of Transformation: Release Lies, Receive
Healing, and Discover Your Empowered Self

By Suzy Holling

COPYRIGHT PAGE

True Self
40 Days of Transformation: Release Lies, Receive Healing, and Discover Your Empowered Self

Suzy Holling Publishing Company.

DEDICATION

This book is dedicated first and foremost to my Papa in heaven and to Jesus, my Lord and Savior. This was Your idea. Because of You, I have been set free and empowered to help others step into greater freedom.

To my husband, Jake, and my children—Trent, Miles, and Avery—thank you from the depths of my heart. I am grateful for your sacrifices, unwavering belief in me, and my greatest cheerleaders.

To my best friends who have believed in me, shared ideas, offered wisdom, and spoken life into me: if you're questioning whether you are one of those friends, YES, you are! I will forever be thankful.

TABLE OF CONTENTS

INTRODUCTION

DEVOTIONAL PAGES

TABLE OF CONTENTS
CONTINUED

BECOMING YOUR TRUE SELF

Imagine waking up each morning with an unshakeable assurance that you are enough. Picture negative thoughts dissipating like morning mist under the sun's warmth. See yourself fully equipped, taking every thought captive, and standing victorious in the unseen battle for your mind.

This 40-day journey is not just about reading—it's about transforming your heart and mind. Each day, you'll let go of what no longer serves you and replace it with the powerful truth of who you are in Christ. God's Word holds life-changing freedom, waiting to break every hidden lie and set you free.

Are you ready to take that step? Many of us unknowingly cling to hidden lies that limit us—beliefs about ourselves, our worth, and even our purpose. They act as invisible chains, holding us back. But God's Word declares that you are a new creation (2 Corinthians 5:17) and that you can do all things through Christ who strengthens you (Philippians 4:13). This journey will help you to demolish those strongholds.

No More Desert Wandering

Just as the Israelites were freed from slavery but spent 40 years wandering in the wilderness, we too can feel stuck—even after being freed from our past. They were physically free yet mentally enslaved, still carrying a "slave mentality." This journey is about breaking that mindset, stepping boldly into your Promised Land. No more wandering in the desert of doubt. Together, we're claiming purpose, clarity, and freedom.

Jesus calls us to go into the world and bring others to freedom (Matthew 28:19-20), but first, we must find it ourselves. True freedom starts here, within our hearts and minds, as we embrace the person God created us to be.

Daily Reflection and Release

As you walk through these 40 days, take each prayer, each declaration, and each truth to heart. Take a moment to ask God if there are lies you've been unknowingly believing—whether consciously or deep within. Often, our biggest breakthroughs come when we realize we've been holding onto things we didn't even know were there.

For example, I recently asked God if I believed I was meant to suffer. I thought I didn't, yet He showed me otherwise. This moment became a revelation: I had unknowingly accepted a mindset of suffering, forgetting that Jesus already suffered for me. His blood is enough. I am called to live in freedom.

Speak the truth aloud. Declare it over your life. Release the lie and receive the truth. Change begins in the heart, and with each new truth, the shift deepens.

Renewing the Mind with Truth
In this devotional, we'll confront 40 common lies that hold people back from living fully in their identity in Christ. These lies are subtle yet powerful, distorting our understanding of God's love and our worth. Together, let's confront these falsehoods, one by one, replacing them with the liberating truth of Scripture.

"We demolish arguments and every pretension that sets itself up against the knowledge of God, and we take captive every thought to make it obedient to Christ" (2 Corinthians 10:5).

Through daily reflections and declarations, God's truth will take root in your heart and mind. Over the next 40 days, I believe something profound will shift within you. Imagine true freedom—worries melting away as security in Christ fills you with joy, peace, and unconditional love. Imagine stepping into the real you, the person God designed, with confidence in your purpose.

The Power of Speaking Truth Over Yourself
When you walk in freedom, you know who you are. There's a joy that nothing —no circumstance, no person—can take away. You're no longer weighed down by fear or doubt but are passionately alive in the calling God has placed on your life.

Closing Declaration
As you journey through these 40 days, remember that you are fully known and fully loved. Just as God transformed the Israelites, He will transform you. Speak the truth aloud and believe it: "I am a child of God, empowered to live fully and freely." Let's step into the Promised Land He has prepared for you.

HOW TO USE THIS DEVOTIONAL

Step 1: Ask God

Each day, ask God if you're holding onto the lie that's being addressed. Before we release something, we need to see it clearly. Spend time with God and ask, "Lord, is there a part of me that believes this?" It might be obvious or hidden deep within, but keep asking and seeking. Imagine addressing "unworthiness." Ask, "Father, do I believe, in any way, that I'm unworthy of love?" Don't rush it. Sometimes God responds with an impression, a feeling, or even through tears. Just sit with it and keep seeking.

Step 2: Release the Lie

Once you've identified a lie, let it go. Picture yourself giving it to God—whether it's "I'm unworthy" or "I'm unloved"—and surrender it at the foot of the cross. Jesus' sacrifice was for you, so release that lie and receive the truth that you are fully worthy of His love. I encourage you to hold your hands open and pray through the release, using the prayers provided as a guide.

Step 3: Receive and Declare the Truth

After releasing the lie, replace it with God's truth and declare it out loud. Scripture tells us that words hold the power of life and death (Proverbs 18:21). So, speak life! Declare, "I am worthy of love. I am of great value." As you speak truth, it rewires your mind, and invites God's power into your life. If we've ever spoken negative words over ourselves, we can ask God to redeem those moments. "Thank You, Jesus, for redeeming my words." Declare your worth daily—your words have power!

The Power of Decrees and Declarations

Many of us are harder on ourselves than anyone else. When I fully grasp how deeply God loves me, it opens the door to healing and clarity in my identity. Speaking decrees aloud helps align us with who God says we are, bringing His truth into our lives. Each time I declare who I am in Christ, I feel His love empowering me to live boldly and confidently. Speaking these truths is a powerful act that brings healing and reinforces our identity as His beloved children.

Step 4: Reflect and Be Restored

Take time to process what God reveals each day. Reflect, journal, pray, and let God's truth sink in. This is where real transformation happens. Write down what's changing within you, and keep a record of the truths God reveals. Declare these truths daily and walk in confidence, knowing that Christ's sacrifice was for you, and that freedom is yours.

The Power of God's Word

God's Word is life-changing, a mirror showing us our true identity. As we declare Scripture over ourselves, we align with God's view, building confidence and resilience. Each verse becomes a weapon to guard against doubt and insecurity, affirming that we're loved, chosen, and empowered.

Come Expectant

What you put into these 40 days will reflect in your transformation. Release the lies, receive the truth, and come with anticipation for what God will do.

Your journey is worth sharing, so please tag @sheiscommissioned on Instagram or join our "True Self" Facebook group—we'd love to walk this path with you. For more information go to www.trueselfdevotional.com

DAY 1: FULLY LOVED

THE LIE: "I HAVE TO EARN GOD'S LOVE" OR "I AM UNLOVABLE"

Beloved, let's begin with a deep breath. As you inhale, allow yourself to feel God's uncontainable, unchanging love flooding over you. His love isn't earned or achieved—it's a boundless gift, freely given to you as His beloved child. Know this: nothing you do can make Him love you more, and nothing can make Him love you less. His love for you is steady, unfailing, and all-encompassing. Let every ounce of that truth settle in, grounding you in His endless embrace.

We often fall into the trap of thinking we have to strive to be perfect, or to perform in a way that wins God's affection. But His love isn't like that—it isn't based on how well we do or how many mistakes we make. His love was demonstrated through Jesus on the cross, long before you could ever try to earn it. "See what great love the Father has lavished on us, that we should be called children of God!" (1 John 3:1) You are fully loved, just as you are, flaws and all.

There are days when we may feel unworthy or distant from this love, when the lie creeps in that we are unlovable. But God's Word speaks a different truth: "For God so loved the world that He gave His one and only Son, that whoever believes in Him shall not perish but have eternal life" (John 3:16). His love for you is beyond comprehension, beyond performance, and beyond any of your failures. His thoughts about you are precious and constant. Psalm 139:17-18 reminds us, "How precious are your thoughts about me, O God! They cannot be numbered; I can't even count them—they outnumber the grains of sand!"

God's love for you is a reality that transcends every fear, every doubt, and every moment when you've felt unloved. The Bible tells us, "I am convinced that nothing can ever separate us from God's love" (Romans 8:38). Nothing—no struggle, no sin, no circumstance—can pull you away from His relentless love. You are held tightly in His embrace, fully seen, fully known, and fully loved.

Declarations - Speak these truths out loud:
I declare that I am fully and infinitely loved by my Father in heaven. I do not have to earn His love; it is freely given to me. I reject the lie that I am unlovable or that I must strive for His affection. I receive the truth that I am deeply cherished just as I am. God's love for me is unconditional, and I rest in the assurance that nothing can separate me from His love.

REFLECT & JOURNAL

Prayer: Heavenly Father, I release the lie that I have to earn Your love or that I am unlovable. Help me to rest in the truth that Your love is constant, unshakable, and freely given. Open my heart to fully receive this love and let it shape my identity as Your beloved child. Thank You for Jesus, who demonstrated the depth of Your love for me. Fill every corner of my heart with Your presence, and help me to live confidently in the knowledge that I am fully and forever loved. In Jesus' name, Amen.

Take a moment to sit quietly and reflect on how you've been striving to earn God's love, or feeling unworthy of it. Write down any thoughts, fears, or doubts that have crept into your mind about being unlovable. Now, write down the truth: that God loves you without condition.

How can you embrace this truth in your everyday life? What steps can you take to stop striving and simply rest in His love? Spend time in gratitude, journaling and thanking Him for His overwhelming, never-ending love for you.

_____

_____

_____

_____

_____

_____

_____

_____

_____

_____

DAY 2: ENOUGH
THE LIE: "I AM NOT ENOUGH"

How often do we feel the weight of not being enough? The lie whispers that we lack the abilities, the strength, or the worth to fulfill the roles and callings placed upon our lives. It seeps into our identity as parents, friends, workers, and children of God. Yet the truth is, we are more than enough because we are created by the God who is **more than enough**.

You are not a mistake or an afterthought. God created you with intention, purpose, and care.

Even in our weaknesses, God's power shines through. 2 Corinthians 12:9 says, "My grace is sufficient for you, for my power is made perfect in weakness." His grace fills the gaps where we fall short, and His strength carries us through every trial.

In Ephesians 2:10, we learn that we are God's handiwork, created to do good works which He prepared in advance. This means that every single role, every calling on your life, has been designed with purpose, and God Himself equips you to fulfill it. When we lean on Him, His strength overcomes our inadequacies.

Declare out loud:
Today, I declare that I am enough because Christ is enough. I am fearfully and wonderfully made. I am equipped, empowered, and loved by God. His grace is more than sufficient to cover my weaknesses, and I trust in His strength within me. I reject feelings of inadequacy and embrace my identity as God's beloved child, created for a purpose.

Prayer:
Heavenly Father, I surrender the feelings of inadequacy and self-doubt that have weighed me down. I release the lie that I am not enough, and I open my heart to Your truth—that in You, I am whole. Your grace is sufficient for me, and Your strength is made perfect in my weakness. Help me to see myself as You see me, empowered to do the good works You have prepared for me. Fill my heart with Your confidence and remind me daily that I am more than enough because You are in me. In Jesus' name, Amen.

REFLECT & JOURNAL

Psalm 139:14 declares, "I praise you because I am fearfully and wonderfully made; your works are wonderful, I know that full well." This is God's declaration over you—He has made you with intention, precision, and love. You were not an accident. You are crafted for "such a time as this" (Esther 4:14). His handiwork in your life is more than enough.

Where in your life have you believed the lie that you are not enough? Take a moment to reflect and write down any areas where you've felt inadequate—whether it's in your relationships, your work, or your spiritual walk. Now, ask God to reveal how His grace is covering each of these areas. What are the unique gifts and strengths He's placed inside of you? Write down one way you can step forward in confidence, knowing that His grace and strength are more than enough. Let His truth fill the space where doubt once lived.

_____

_____

_____

_____

_____

_____

_____

_____

_____

_____

_____

_____

DAY 3: SALVATION

THE LIE: "AM I SAVED?"

One of the most pivotal moments in my Christian journey was realizing that I was, indeed, saved. Growing up, I often responded to every altar call, praying to receive the Lord repeatedly, unsure if it had "stuck." I didn't have a dramatic, life-altering experience when I first accepted Jesus as my Savior, and because of that, I doubted whether my salvation was real. I wanted the emotional "feeling" to accompany my decision, but it never came.

It wasn't until later, in college, when I truly grasped the depth of my salvation through Scripture. I read the verses below, and they brought a deep assurance that transformed my heart. My confidence in walking with the Lord was forever changed, and I knew with certainty that I was saved.

1 John 5:11-13 says, "And this is the testimony: God has given us eternal life, and this life is in His Son. Whoever has the Son has life; whoever does not have the Son of God does not have life. I write these things to you who believe in the name of the Son of God so that you may know that you have eternal life."

Have you ever doubted your salvation because you didn't have a big emotional experience or a life-changing moment when you first accepted Jesus? Do you sometimes feel that because of your past, salvation may not be for you?

Prayer:
Lord, I thank You and praise You for the assurance of my salvation. I am grateful that Jesus lives in me and that, through Him, I have eternal life. Help me to rest confidently in Your promise, knowing that my name is written in the Lamb's Book of Life. I trust You, Lord, and I know that I am saved through the finished work of Jesus. Thank You, Jesus, for the gift of salvation. Amen.

Declare out loud:
I believe in the name of the Son of God. I am saved, not by works, but by grace through faith in Jesus Christ. I have eternal life because I have Jesus living in me. My salvation is secure, and my name is written in the Lamb's Book of Life. I rest in the assurance that I am a child of God, fully loved and saved.

REFLECT & JOURNAL

Take a moment today to meditate on the truth of these words. If you've ever doubted, know that God's Word is clear—you are saved if you believe in His Son. Walk in the assurance that His promises are unshakable.

Other scripture I love about salvation is Joel 2:32 and John 3:16.

If you've ever questioned whether you're truly saved, let today be the day you stand firm in God's Word. Your salvation is not based on how you feel or on your past. It is based on the unchanging truth that when you have the Son, you have life—eternal life. Walk confidently in this truth, knowing that you are secure in His love. Amen.

*There is a prayer at the end of this book if you are seeking salvation. As believers He does call us into repentance and to confess that He is Lord.

_____

_____

_____

_____

_____

_____

_____

_____

_____

_____

_____

_____

DAY 4: HEARING

THE LIE: "I CAN'T HEAR FROM GOD"

Have you ever wondered if God is truly speaking to you? Many of us grapple with the belief that we cannot hear from Him, thinking His voice is reserved for those deemed more spiritual or faithful. But the truth is that God longs to communicate with you personally; His voice is not distant or unreachable. As His children, we are created to hear Him.

In 1 Kings 19:11-12, Elijah sought God in a time of desperation. While expecting Him to come through loud, dramatic events, he found God in a gentle whisper. Elijah had to quiet himself to truly hear God's voice. Similarly, Jesus reassures us in John 10:27, "My sheep listen to my voice; I know them, and they follow me." If you belong to Him, you are designed to hear His voice, whether through scripture, prayer, dreams, or wise counsel.

Prayer:
Heavenly Father, I release the lie that I cannot hear from You. I believe Your Word, which says I am Your sheep and can hear Your voice. Help me tune out distractions and recognize the many ways You speak to me—whether through scripture, a quiet whisper, or the wise counsel of others. Open the ears of my heart to receive Your words, and help me trust that You are always near, ready to guide me. I embrace the truth that I am designed to hear from You. In Jesus' name, Amen.

Declare out loud:
I decree and declare that I am attuned to the voice of my Heavenly Father, and I hear Him clearly. I decree that God speaks to me in unique ways, and I am receptive to His whispers. I will hear God's voice through scripture, prayer, worship, and wise counsel. I decree that God is always speaking, and I am always listening with a heart open to His leading.

"My sheep listen to my voice; I know them, and they follow me" (John 10:27).

"...After the fire came a gentle whisper" (1 Kings 19:11-12).

"Call to me, and I will answer you and tell you great and unsearchable things you do not know" (Jeremiah 33:3).

God speaks to each of us differently, whether it's a gentle whisper, a scripture, or through the voice of a friend. The key is to stay open and receptive, trusting that He is always near, ready to communicate His heart to you. Just today a bald eagle flew over me bringing me a strong sense of peace with a decision I just made. God may speak from any form.

Let this truth settle in your heart today—you can hear from God. Keep listening. He's speaking, and He has incredible things to share with you.

Write down specific ways you have heard from God in the past. How can you create space in your life to be more attuned to His voice? Reflect on your experiences and ask God for clarity in hearing Him moving forward.

_____

_____

_____

_____

_____

_____

_____

_____

_____

_____

YOU CAN HEAR

DAY 5: FORGIVEN
THE LIE: "I DON'T DESERVE FORGIVENESS"

Beloved, do you ever feel like your mistakes are too big, too shameful to be forgiven? Does the weight of guilt, or regret make you feel unworthy of redemption? These lies can be crippling, but they are not the truth. Jesus went to the cross because of His great love for you. When we refuse to accept His forgiveness, we undermine the incredible power of His sacrifice.

God's Word assures us that His forgiveness is not something we earn—it is a gift, freely given through the blood of Jesus. "If we confess our sins, He is faithful and just to forgive us our sins and purify us from all unrighteousness" (1 John 1:9). This forgiveness is not based on our worthiness, but on His grace and mercy. No matter how deep your shame or how great your sins, God remembers them no more. "I, even I, am He who blots out your transgressions, for my own sake, and remembers your sins no more" (Isaiah 43:25).

Think of the story of the prodigal son (Luke 15:11-32), who wasted his inheritance and returned home feeling unworthy. But his father didn't reject him. He ran to him with love, open arms, and a heart full of forgiveness. This is the picture of God's love for you. No matter how far you've strayed, He welcomes you back with joy, <u>forgiving every mistake</u>.

God's forgiveness is complete and final. "As far as the east is from the west, so far has He removed our transgressions from us" (Psalm 103:12). His grace covers all our sins, wiping the slate clean. You are forgiven, not because you deserve it, but because God loves you and sent His Son to pay the price for your redemption.

Declare out loud:
I declare that I am fully forgiven through the blood of Jesus. I release the lie that I am unforgivable or that I must earn God's forgiveness. I receive the truth that I am cleansed, loved, and set free from all shame and guilt. I am no longer defined by my past, but by God's grace. His forgiveness covers me completely, and I walk in freedom. I am at peace with being forgiven.

REFLECT & JOURNAL

Prayer:
Heavenly Father, I release the lie that I am too broken or sinful to be forgiven. I confess my sins and embrace the truth of Your complete forgiveness. Thank You for the cross, for the sacrifice of Jesus, which cleanses me from all unrighteousness. Help me to fully embrace this truth, letting go of guilt, shame, and condemnation. I choose to forgive those who have wronged me, trusting in Your justice and grace. Thank You for the gift of freedom that comes through Your love. In Jesus' name, Amen.

Take a moment to reflect on any area of your life where you've struggled to accept God's forgiveness. Are there sins, regrets, or mistakes that you've been holding onto, believing they are unforgivable? Write them down and surrender them to God. Now, think about those you need to forgive. What grudges or hurts have kept you from experiencing true freedom? Remember, you are fully forgiven, fully loved, and fully free.

_____

_____

_____

_____

_____

_____

_____

_____

_____

_____

_____

DAY 6: ACCEPTED

THE LIE: "I HAVE TO BE PERFECT TO BE ACCEPTED"

"But He said to me, 'My grace is sufficient for you, for my power is made perfect in weakness.' Therefore I will boast all the more gladly about my weaknesses, so that Christ's power may rest on me" (2 Corinthians 12:9).

We often fall into the trap of believing that we must be perfect to be accepted by God or others. This lie can weigh us down, causing us to strive endlessly for an unattainable standard. But the truth is that God does not require our perfection—He calls us to rest in His grace. His love for us is not based on our ability to be flawless, but on the work that Jesus did on the cross. Through Christ, we are already accepted.

Job was a man who lived blamelessly before God, yet he endured tremendous suffering. In his pain, Job felt abandoned by God and questioned why he was facing such hardship. Despite his confusion and sense of rejection, Job ultimately learned that God's acceptance and love were not dependent on his circumstances or perfection. God reminded Job of His infinite wisdom and care, showing that He was always present, even when Job couldn't see it. Like Job, we may feel abandoned or unworthy, but God's acceptance isn't based on our strength—it's grounded in His love for us, even in our weakest moments.

Declare out loud:
I release the lie that I have to be perfect to be accepted. I receive the truth that God's grace is enough for me, and in my weakness, His strength is made perfect. I am accepted and loved just as I am.

Prayer:
Heavenly Father, I release the pressure to be perfect. I surrender the lie that I must meet impossible standards to be loved and accepted. I receive Your grace that is more than enough for me. Help me to rest in the truth that I am accepted because of what Jesus has done, not what I can achieve. Thank You for loving me unconditionally. In Jesus' name, Amen.

REFLECT & JOURNAL

"Come to me, all you who are weary and burdened, and I will give you rest" (Matthew 11:28).

Where in your life have you been striving for perfection in order to feel accepted? Where have you felt abandoned? Take time today to reflect on God's grace and how it frees you from the need to be perfect. Let His love cover your imperfections and give you peace.

_____

_____

_____

_____

_____

_____

_____

_____

_____

_____

_____

_____

_____

DAY 7: ALONE

THE LIE: "I AM ALL ALONE"

Beloved, there are times when the weight of life's struggles can make us feel utterly alone, like no one truly understands the depth of our pain. Loneliness can creep in, filling our hearts with isolation and disconnection. But today, we confront this lie head-on and remind ourselves of the unshakable truth—you are <u>never</u> alone.

In those moments when life feels overwhelming and you believe no one understands, remember this: God is not only present with you, He goes before you. Deuteronomy 31:8 declares, "The Lord himself goes before you and will be with you; he will never leave you nor forsake you." Even when you can't feel His presence, He is walking with you, holding you up, and guiding you through.

The Holy Spirit, our divine Helper, resides within us, comforting, guiding, and empowering us. John 14:26 reminds us that the Holy Spirit "will teach you all things and will remind you of everything I have said to you." You are not navigating life alone—God's very Spirit dwells within you, offering strength in your weakness and companionship in your solitude.

Declare out loud:
I declare that I am never alone. God is with me through every challenge, sorrow, and season of life. I reject the lie that I walk this journey by myself. Jesus is my constant companion, and I receive His truth that He will never leave me nor forsake me. Loneliness has no power over me, for I am cherished and enveloped in God's unending presence.

Prayer:
Heavenly Father, I come before You today, acknowledging my feelings of loneliness and isolation. I release the lie that I am alone, and I receive the truth that You are always with me. Thank You for the Holy Spirit, my constant companion, who strengthens and comforts me in every situation. Help me to feel Your presence in moments of struggle, and remind me daily that You will never leave me nor forsake me. Thank You for Your unfailing love that surrounds me. In Jesus' name, Amen.

REFLECT & JOURNAL

God sees every tear, knows every sorrow, and remains steadfastly by your side. Psalm 56:8 tells us, "You have kept count of my tossings; put my tears in your bottle. Are they not in your book?" Every tear, every sleepless night, is seen and held by God.

And in Matthew 28:20, Jesus promises, "I am with you always, even to the very end of the age." This promise speaks directly to the heart of loneliness —we are never abandoned. He is with us always, through every storm, every valley, every trial.

Where have you felt alone in your life? Take a moment to reflect on how God's presence has been with you all along, even in the times when you couldn't see it. How can you actively remind yourself of His constant companionship? Write down specific ways you can turn to the Holy Spirit for guidance and comfort, and take time to thank God for never abandoning you. Embrace His love today, and rest in the truth that you are **never** alone.

_____

_____

_____

_____

_____

_____

_____

_____

DAY 8: PEACE
THE LIE: "I'LL NEVER FIND PEACE"

Today, we embark on a journey to claim the peace that Jesus promised us. Life's pressures may make peace feel out of reach, but God's Word assures us that we are meant to walk in a peace that surpasses all understanding. Let's explore Scripture, pour our hearts into prayer, and declare that peace is not merely a promise—it is our inheritance.

In John 14:27, Jesus says, "Peace I leave with you; my peace I give you. I do not give to you as the world gives. Do not let your hearts be troubled and do not be afraid." Jesus has given us His peace to embrace and He already lives within us. A peace that surpasses all understanding (Phil 4:7).

Prayer:
Heavenly Father, I come before You today, seeking Your peace to fill my heart. I release every anxiety, worry, and fear that has taken hold of me, surrendering them to You. I open my heart to receive the peace You promised—a peace that calms every storm. Help me rest in Your presence and trust in Your goodness, knowing that Your peace surpasses all understanding. In Jesus' mighty name, I pray. Amen.

Declare out loud:
I speak shalom peace over myself right now. I decree that the peace Jesus gave me is alive in my heart and mind, and I declare that I carry God's peace wherever I go. My heart remains steady, anchored in God's peace, regardless of my circumstances. Fear and anxiety have no hold on me, for the peace of Christ surrounds and fills me. I decree that my life reflects God's peace, drawing others to the Prince of Peace.

Beloved, take a deep breath and let the peace of Jesus fill your soul. Remember, peace isn't just a feeling—it's a gift that is already yours. No matter the storms around you, Christ's peace dwells within you. Walk confidently today, knowing that true peace resides in your heart and that through you, others will witness His calming presence.

REFLECT & JOURNAL

Philippians 4:6-7 encourages us not to be anxious about anything, but to present our requests to God, assuring us that His peace will guard our hearts and minds. Additionally, Isaiah 26:3 states, "You will keep in perfect peace those whose minds are steadfast because they trust in you." Trusting God leads to an unshakeable peace that carries us through life's challenges.

Consider the areas in your life where you feel anxious or troubled. How can you invite God's peace into those situations? Journal about your struggles right now, and reflect on the ways God has provided peace in your past.

_____

_____

_____

_____

_____

_____

_____

_____

_____

_____

_____

_____

_____

DAY 9: IDENTITY

THE LIE: "I DON'T KNOW WHO I AM"

Have you ever felt lost, or unsure of your true identity? Many of us grapple with defining ourselves by what we do, the roles we play, or how others perceive us. This uncertainty can leave us questioning, "Who am I?" But God wants you to find your identity firmly rooted in Him. You are His beloved child, defined not by your past or mistakes but by His love and truth.

When Moses struggled with his identity in Exodus 3, God called him from the burning bush and reminded him of his purpose: to be a leader and deliverer. Despite Moses' doubts, God's promise was clear: "I will be with you." Just as God assured Moses, He assures you that His presence affirms your true identity and gives you strength.

1 John 3:2 says, "Dear friends, now we are children of God, and what we will be has not yet been made known. But we know that when Christ appears, we shall be like Him." You are a child of God, and while the fullness of your identity may not yet be revealed, you can confidently embrace who you are through Christ.

Prayer:
Gracious Father, I come to You as Your beloved child. I release the lie that I don't know who I am and choose to embrace the truth that I am cherished and loved. Forgive me for doubting my identity in You. Fill me with a deeper understanding of my divine identity as Your beloved child. Guide me to live fully in this truth. In Jesus' name, Amen.

Declare out loud:
I release the lie that I don't know who I am, and I embrace the truth that I am who God says I am. I am chosen, loved, and approved by Him. I refuse to let my past or others' opinions define me. I trust in God's purpose for my life and walk confidently in my identity. I am a daughter/son of the King, anointed and appointed for His purpose. I am a Royal Priest called by name. My identity is rooted in Christ, and I live confidently as His beloved.

REFLECT & JOURNAL

Consider what defines you. Have you sought your identity in others' opinions or past mistakes? Shift your focus to God's truth: you are His child, completely chosen and loved. Rest in this truth and ask God to reveal more of your divine identity each day. Write down how God sees you as His cherished one, and reflect on how that impacts your life.

Scriptures to meditate on: 1 John 3:2, Galatians 4:7, Ephesians 2:10

Remember, God has called you His own. Embrace your true identity. You belong to Him!

_____

_____

_____

_____

_____

_____

_____

_____

_____

_____

_____

_____

_____

_____

DAY 10: THOUGHTS
THE LIE: "I CAN'T CONTROL MY THOUGHTS"

We've all experienced moments where our thoughts seem uncontrollable, leaving us feeling powerless. The lie that says we cannot control our thoughts often makes us feel stuck in negativity or fear. But the truth is, through Christ, we have the power to take control of our minds and align our thoughts with God's truth.

The Bible teaches us that what we think shapes who we are: "As a man thinketh in his heart, so is he" (Proverbs 23:7). God has given us the ability to renew our minds, so we are not bound by thoughts of failure, unworthiness, or fear.

Even Paul, a great apostle, struggled with his inner conflict, wanting to do right but falling into sin. He laments, "For I do not do the good I want to do, but the evil I do not want to do—this I keep on doing" (Romans 7:19). Yet, he finds hope in Christ, realizing that through Him, he can be free from this inner struggle. This passage reminds us that God empowers us to overcome our thoughts (and therefore actions) through His Spirit.

Prayer:
Heavenly Father, I release the lie that I have no control over my thoughts. I receive Your truth that, through Your Spirit, I have the mind of Christ. Help me to take every thought captive and submit it to Your will. Guide me as I renew my mind daily, filling my thoughts with Your love, peace, and truth. In Jesus' name, Amen.

Declare out loud:
I declare that I release the lie that I cannot control my thoughts. I receive the truth that I have the mind of Christ and am empowered by the Holy Spirit. My thoughts are being renewed by God's truth, and I choose to focus on what is true, pure, and lovely. I set my mind on the Spirit, which brings life and peace, and I reject the mindset of the flesh, which leads to death.

REFLECT & JOURNAL

Romans 12:2 tells us that by renewing our minds, we can experience transformation and understand God's will for our lives. This renewal is not something we do alone—the Holy Spirit is our guide, giving us the mind of Christ and empowering us to think on things that are true, pure, and lovely (Philippians 4:8).

Through the Holy Spirit, you have access to self-control and the ability to guide your thoughts, no matter how overwhelming they may feel. Scripture reminds us that we can "take every thought captive to make it obedient to Christ" (2 Corinthians 10:5). The lie that your thoughts are beyond your control keeps you in a place of defeat, but God's truth sets you free to think, believe, and act from a place of peace.

As you reflect, ask yourself:
What kinds of thoughts or patterns do I struggle to control? Are they rooted in fear, insecurity, or discouragement? Journal how would my life change if I truly believed that I can bring these thoughts into alignment with His truth?

_____

_____

_____

_____

_____

_____

_____

_____

_____

DAY 11: WORTH

THE LIE: "MY WORTH IS BASED ON WHAT I DO"

God talks to us in different ways like I explained at the beginning of this devotional. He speaks to me with songs often. The lyrics of "You Are Wanted" by Dara MacLean echo in my heart, reminding me that your worth is not determined by your achievements, but by the love of the Creator who formed you. God doesn't value us based on our performance or what we accomplish—He values us because He created us with love and purpose.

Jesus tells the parable of the lost sheep to show God's heart toward those who feel lost or unworthy. In the story, the shepherd leaves the ninety-nine sheep to go after the one that wandered off. Even though that one sheep had nothing to offer, the shepherd pursued it with relentless love.

The sheep didn't have to do anything to earn the shepherd's attention—it was wanted and valued just because it belonged to him. This parable reminds us that we are deeply wanted and loved by God, not because of what we've done, but because we are His creation.

Prayer:
Lord, I release the lie that my worth is based on my performance or accomplishments. I receive Your truth that my value is rooted in Your love for me. Help me to see myself through Your eyes, as Your beloved creation, chosen and cherished. I open my heart to Your affirmation, knowing that my worth is secure in being Yours. Thank You for redeeming me and calling me by name. In Jesus' name, Amen.

Declare out loud:
I declare that I am worthy, not because of what I do, but because of who God says I am. I am loved deeply and unconditionally by my Creator. I receive the truth that I am honored, exceptional, and valued beyond measure. My worth is not based on my performance, but on God's love and purpose for my life. I am welcomed and cherished as His beloved child.

REFLECT & JOURNAL

Isaiah 43:1 beautifully captures this truth:
"But now, this is what the Lord says—he who created you, [Your Name], he who formed you, [Your Name]: 'Do not fear, for I have redeemed you; I have called you by name, you are mine.'"

Let that sink in. God created you. He formed you with intention. He has redeemed you, and He knows you by name. You are His. This means your worth is immeasurable because it is based on who He is, not what you do.

Take a moment to reflect on where you have tied your worth to performance or achievements. Now, invite God's truth into those spaces. How does it feel to know that your worth is anchored in God's love for you, not in what you do? Journal your thoughts, and let this be a time of releasing the pressure to perform, while embracing the truth that you are wanted, chosen, and loved by God.

_____

_____

_____

_____

_____

_____

_____

_____

_____

_____

DAY 12: PURPOSE
THE LIE: "I HAVE NO PURPOSE"

You are here by divine design, crafted with a purpose that is uniquely yours. Let the words of Jeremiah 1:5 resonate deeply: "Before you even took your first breath, God knew you—intimately and purposefully." Imagine that! Long before you faced any of life's struggles or successes, God had already dreamed up a beautiful purpose for you—a calling that brings His glory to life through your story.

This calling isn't limited to just a few; purpose is woven into the fabric of every soul He creates. Yes, including you! You carry within you a divine destiny, one that was set in motion from the beginning. God's vision for you is unlike anyone else's. He has placed dreams in your heart, passions in your spirit, and strengths that only you possess.

Look at Gideon's story in Judges 6. When God called him to rise up and lead Israel against powerful enemies, Gideon was hiding, filled with doubts about who he was and why he mattered. He saw himself as insignificant, the least of his family, and unfit for greatness. But God met him right there, in the midst of his insecurities, and spoke words that transformed everything: "Go in the strength you have... I will be with you." God didn't see Gideon's fears; He saw Gideon's potential. And He equipped him for a purpose only Gideon could fulfill.

In the same way, God has appointed you for a purpose that only you can live out. The dreams stirring in your heart? They're not random; they're divine hints toward the life He has called you to. He has crafted every detail, shaping your heart, your gifts, and even your challenges, to prepare you for a destiny that will impact the world around you.

Declare out loud:
I declare that I am created with a purpose. God Himself has called me, and I step forward with confidence, knowing a promised land of destiny awaits me. I reject every lie that says I am without purpose—I am a deliberate creation, made for God's glory.

REFLECT & JOURNAL

Prayer

Lord, today I release the lie that I have no purpose. I surrender any feelings of inadequacy, fear, or doubt that try to overshadow Your truth. I receive the reality that You purposed me from the beginning of time and that I am a masterpiece in Your hands. Guide me as I trust in the dreams You've placed in my heart, knowing they are part of Your design. Thank You for the purpose and calling that await me. In Jesus' name, Amen.

How can you trust more deeply in the purpose God has for you, even when life feels uncertain? What dreams or desires in your heart might be nudging you toward His calling? Journal what you envision in your future, knowing that dream is intentional—it's on purpose.

_____

_____

_____

_____

_____

_____

_____

_____

_____

_____

_____

_____

_____

DAY 13: WORDS

THE LIE: "I HAVE NO CONTROL OVER MY WORDS"

When God spoke the universe into existence, He demonstrated the incredible power of words. As believers, we carry that same authority within us because the Holy Spirit dwells in us. This means that when you speak, your words carry weight—they have the power to create and shape reality.

Think about how Jesus used words throughout His ministry. He healed the sick, raised the dead, and cast out demons—all through His spoken declarations. His words brought life where there was death, healing where there was sickness, and hope where there was despair. The Bible tells us in Proverbs 18:21 that "The tongue has the power of life and death." Our words can build up or tear down, create or destroy.

Sometimes it feels like we have no control over our words, especially in moments of frustration, fear, or stress. But this is a lie. Through Christ, we have the power to choose life-giving words. When we speak, we are shaping the atmosphere around us. If I say, "This is impossible," I am empowering that struggle to grow. But if I declare, "With God, all things are possible," I am inviting His power into the situation.

God has given us the ability to control our words, and as we surrender our tongues to Him, we can speak life, hope, and truth over ourselves and others.

Prayer:
Lord, I ask for Your help in controlling my words. I release the lie that I have no control over what I say, and I receive the truth that through Your Spirit, I have the power to speak life, truth, and hope. Guard my tongue, Lord, and help me to use it for Your glory. Let my words bring life to every situation, and may they always reflect Your love, grace, and promises. I surrender my speech to You, trusting that You will guide my tongue to build up and not tear down. Amen.

Declare out loud:
Today, I declare that I have control over my words. I choose to speak life, hope, and truth over every situation in my life. My words carry the power of God's authority and create positive change. I speak blessings over my challenges and declare that God's promises are true for me.

REFLECT & JOURNAL

"Set a guard over my mouth, Lord; keep watch over the door of my lips" (Psalm 141:3).

"The tongue has the power of life and death, and those who love it will eat its fruit" (Proverbs 18:21).

Take a moment to reflect on the words you speak regularly. Do your words align with God's truth, or are they more influenced by doubt, fear, or negativity? Our words hold creative power. What would happen if you started using that power to build up your life and the lives of those around you? Imagine the transformation that could take place when you choose to declare God's promises and hope over every challenge you face.

Journal your thoughts on the power of your words.

_____

_____

_____

_____

_____

_____

_____

_____

_____

_____

_____

_____

DAY 14: ACCEPTED
THE LIE: "GOD IS MAD AT ME"

Have you ever felt like God is angry with you? Maybe because of mistakes you've made or because you feel unworthy of His love. This can make us feel distant from God. But let me assure you, God's love and mercy are far greater than any mistakes we make. He is not a God who holds grudges, but a God of grace, who desires to draw us closer to Him despite our shortcomings.

A great example of someone who believed "God is mad at me" is Jonah. After fleeing from God's command to preach in Nineveh, Jonah found himself caught in a violent storm. He believed his disobedience brought God's anger and told the sailors to throw him overboard. But instead of punishing Jonah, God sent a great fish to save him (Jonah 1:1-17). This shows that even when we run from God, He pursues us with mercy and gives us another chance, not in anger but in grace.

Even when we feel we've fallen short, God's heart is full of mercy. Psalm 103:8-12 reminds us, "The Lord is compassionate and gracious, slow to anger, abounding in love... as far as the east is from the west, so far has he removed our transgressions." This truth dispels the lie that God is angry, showing instead His compassion, grace, and readiness to forgive.

Prayer:
Father, I come before You today with a humble heart. I release the lie both consciously and subconsciously that You are distant and angry with me, it has kept me from fully embracing Your love. Today, I choose to believe the truth that You welcome me unconditionally with open arms. Forgive me for doubting Your love. Help me to see You as a loving Father who delights in me, even when I stumble. Thank You for Your patience and grace. I receive Your forgiveness and Your unconditional love today, in Jesus' name, Amen.

Declare out loud:
I am not forsaken; God welcomes me with open arms. I am loved, forgiven, and welcomed into God's presence. God's grace covers my mistakes, and His love restores me. I decree that the lie of "God is mad at me" has no power over my life. I am welcomed, forgiven, and loved unconditionally. God's grace is my covering, and His love is my strength.

REFLECT & JOURNAL

Take a moment to reflect on how the lie that "God is mad at me" has affected your relationship with Him. Have you distanced yourself from God out of fear of His anger? Now, picture God as your loving Father, who runs to meet his child with open arms. This is how God responds to us when we turn back to Him, no matter what we've done.

Rest in this truth today, and know that God's love is constant, even in your moments of weakness. You are His, and He welcomes you unconditionally.

Journal where you have felt abandoned and how you can receive today that you are accepted.

_____

_____

_____

_____

_____

_____

_____

_____

_____

_____

_____

_____

_____

DAY 15: FORGIVENESS
THE LIE: "I CAN'T FORGIVE MYSELF"

Are you struggling to forgive yourself? How often do we allow our mistakes to define us, becoming trapped in guilt and shame? That heaviness can feel suffocating, leading us to believe we're unworthy of grace. For me, embracing self-forgiveness transformed my life completely.

Here is a liberating truth: God has already forgiven us through Jesus Christ. When we hold onto unforgiveness, we hinder our ability to experience the fullness of His grace. Forgiveness isn't just a gift we receive; it's also a choice we must actively make. The Lord teaches us in Matthew 6:14 that if we want to be forgiven, we must also forgive others—and that includes forgiving ourselves.

Consider the story of the woman caught in adultery (John 8:1-11). The religious leaders brought her before Jesus, ready to condemn. Instead of judgment, Jesus offered grace, saying, "Has no one condemned you?... Then neither do I condemn you. Go now and leave your life of sin." He acknowledged her sin but extended forgiveness, encouraging her to choose a new path. This powerful act reminds us that even when we fall, we can rise again.

Prayer:
Heavenly Father, I release the burden of feeling like I can't forgive myself. I recognize that my inability to forgive myself keeps me from fully experiencing Your love and grace. I choose to forgive myself for the mistakes I've made, just as You have forgiven me. Help me to remember that Your grace is sufficient and that I am worthy of Your forgiveness. Thank You for setting me free from guilt and shame. In Jesus' name, Amen.

Declare out loud:
I declare that God has forgiven me, and I choose to walk in that forgiveness. I am no longer defined by my past mistakes; I am set free by the grace of Jesus Christ. I forgive myself as God has already forgiven me, releasing guilt and shame. I walk forward in freedom, leaving behind the weight of unforgiveness. I declare that my past no longer holds power over me—I am forgiven, loved, and redeemed. I am empowered by God's forgiveness to rise above my failures and live in His love. I declare that through Christ, I am free to live a new life, filled with grace and purpose.

REFLECT & JOURNAL

What mistakes or choices have you been holding onto, believing you cannot forgive yourself? Spend a moment in prayer, inviting God to shine His light on those burdens. Reflect on the promise of His forgiveness and consider how releasing that burden can lead you to greater freedom. Remember, forgiveness is a precious gift from God.

"I, even I, am He who blots out your transgressions, for my own sake, and remembers your sins no more" (Isaiah 43:25).

By forgiving yourself, you open the door to fully live in His grace and embrace the new life He has for you.

Allow yourself to experience the transformative power of forgiveness today. You are not defined by your past; you are defined by the love and grace of God, who sees you as His beloved child. Journal your raw thoughts below right now.

_____

_____

_____

_____

_____

_____

_____

_____

_____

_____

_____

DAY 16: HOPE

THE LIE: "I HAVE NOTHING TO HOPE FOR"

Have you ever felt hopeless, believing there's nothing left to look forward to? Hopelessness often takes hold when we focus on our circumstances or fall into a victim mindset. I've been there too, tempted to give up hope, thinking, "Why try if disappointment is certain?" But that's not God's plan. He calls us to lift our eyes to Him, the true source of hope.

When we focus on Christ instead of our fears, "failure" becomes an opportunity to grow, not a reason to quit. Like a child learning to walk, falling is part of building strength. In Christ, we always have hope because He is faithful and His plans are good.

Abraham is a powerful example of hope in God's promises. Despite his old age and Sarah's inability to conceive, Abraham "hoped against hope" and trusted in God's word that he would be the father of many nations. Romans 4:18-21 shows that Abraham didn't focus on his impossible circumstances; instead, he trusted in God's power.

Psalm 39:7 declares, "My only hope is in You." When we place our hope in God, we will always have something to look forward to because He is working all things for our good.

Prayer:
Lord, I release the lie that I have nothing to hope for. I ask You to fill my heart with the truth that You are the source of all hope. Take away any despair and help me see my future through Your eyes. Shift my mindset from fear and disappointment to optimism and faith in Your promises. Thank You for the hope and future You have for me. I trust in Your perfect plans and receive Your hope today. Amen.

Declare out loud:
I speak a new hope over my life and mindset. I receive the hope of the Lord and choose to fix my eyes on Jesus, the author and perfecter of my faith. I trust in God's promises and know that He is using every challenge for my growth and good. I declare that my future is secure in Christ, and I am filled with hope and expectation for what He has in store.

REFLECT & JOURNAL

"Love bears all things, believes all things, hopes all things, endures all things" (1 Corinthians 13:7).

"Though outwardly we are wasting away, inwardly we are being renewed day by day" (2 Corinthians 4:16-18).

"But those who hope in the Lord will renew their strength; they will soar on wings like eagles" (Isaiah 40:31).

Reflect on God's promises. How can you shift your mindset to one filled with hope and trust in Him? Write down any fears or disappointments that may be holding you back from embracing the future God has for you.

_____

_____

_____

_____

_____

_____

_____

_____

_____

_____

_____

_____

_____

_____

DAY 17: REDEMPTION

THE LIE: "GOD IS PUNISHING ME FOR MY PAST"

There was a time when I believed this lie deeply. After my first pregnancy ended in miscarriage, I was convinced God was punishing me for my past sin. Guilt overwhelmed me, and I felt trapped in shame. But the truth is, I wasn't being punished. While there are natural consequences to our actions, God doesn't hold our sins against us when we seek forgiveness.

Have you ever found yourself believing that God is punishing you for your mistakes? It's a heavy burden, and Jesus died on the cross to carry it for you. God is not a harsh judge waiting to inflict pain for your past. He is a loving Father who longs to restore, redeem, and heal. Jesus took the punishment for our sins on the cross. When we carry the weight of guilt, we forget that His grace is greater than our past. I do want to mention we are called into repentance - but the redeeming power of the cross was not for punishment.

It's important to ask yourself: Are you holding onto guilt or believing that God is withholding His goodness from you? Release that belief. God's business is not punishment, but redemption. His love covers your past mistakes.

Romans 8:1 says, "There is now no condemnation for those who are in Christ Jesus."

Prayer:
Father, I release the lie that You are punishing me for my past. Help me to fully receive Your grace and forgiveness. Remind me that Jesus paid the price for my sins and I no longer need to carry the weight of guilt. Thank You for redeeming my mistakes and restoring me. I embrace the freedom You offer. In Jesus' name, Amen.

Declare out loud:
I declare that I am free from the burden of guilt and shame. I refuse to believe that God is punishing me for my past. I am redeemed, forgiven, and my sins are forgotten. God's love and mercy surrounds me, and I walk in the freedom that Christ purchased for me.

REFLECT & JOURNAL

Isaiah 43:25 reminds us, "I am He who blots out your transgressions, for my own sake, and remembers your sins no more." Psalm 103:10-12 beautifully states, "He does not treat us as our sins deserve. As far as the east is from the west, so far has He removed our transgressions from us."

Take some time to reflect on areas of your life where you might still feel guilt or fear of punishment. Are there moments from your past that you feel are still weighing you down? Write about how you can embrace God's truth and let go of the lie. Let His grace wash over you today, knowing you are forgiven and free.

Take a moment to journal your thoughts on redemption.

_____

_____

_____

_____

_____

_____

_____

_____

_____

_____

_____

_____

_____

_____

DAY 18: FEAR

THE LIE: "I'LL NEVER OVERCOME MY FEARS"

Fear can be paralyzing, convincing us that we're too weak or stuck to move forward. Whether it's the fear of failure, rejection, or the unknown, it can feel like an insurmountable obstacle. The enemy uses fear to keep us in a cycle of stagnation, but God calls us to rise up in faith and boldness.

You may have tried to push past your fears, only to have them creep back in, making it seem like they control your life. But here's the powerful truth: Fear loses its grip in the presence of God's love. He is right there with you, and His strength will carry you through every challenge. Just as David confronted Goliath with unwavering faith in God's power, you too can stand tall against your fears, knowing that God fights alongside you.

In 1 Samuel 17, young David faced the giant Goliath while everyone else cowered in fear. His power didn't come from his size or experience but from his deep faith. David boldly declared that the same God who delivered him from lions and bears would rescue him from Goliath. With that confidence, he triumphed over the giant. Similarly, God equips us with the strength to conquer our own giants of fear.

So, let me pause and emphasize this truth: You can do it. Embrace your courage, face your battles head-on, and trust in God's unwavering support. You are stronger than you think!

Prayer:
Lord, I release the lie that I can't overcome my fears. Fill me with Your peace and remind me that I am never alone. Help me trust in Your power to face every fear with courage. I give You my anxieties, knowing You care for me. Thank You for Your strength in my weakness. Today, I choose to walk in the boldness and peace You provide. In Jesus' name, Amen.

Declare out loud:
I release fear and anxiety, and I choose faith. I trust in God's power to help me overcome every fear that comes my way. I walk in peace, not in fear, because Jesus has given me His peace. I can face giants because God is with me, and I am fearless because He is my strength.

REFLECT & JOURNAL

What fears have been holding you back? Think on how God's strength and love is greater than your fear. How can you shift your focus from the fear itself to God's promises? Just like David, whose confidence was in God, you too can face your giants. Write down one fear you're ready to release to God today, and ask Him for the strength to overcome it.

Scriptures to reflect on;
Isaiah 41:10, 1 Peter 5:7, John 14:27, 2 Timothy 1:7

Remember, fear is no match for the love and power of God. Step out in faith today!

Journal about something you have been afraid of, that you can step into Gods love, and give to Him today.

_____

_____

_____

_____

_____

_____

_____

_____

_____

_____

_____

_____

_____

DAY 19: PRAYER

THE LIE: "GOD DOESN'T HEAR MY PRAYERS"

There are moments when we feel like our prayers are bouncing off the ceiling, as if God is silent and distant. It's easy to fall into the lie that He doesn't hear us or that He is uninterested in our struggles. But the truth is, God hears every word we pray, and He listens with a loving heart.

The silence we sometimes experience doesn't mean He is absent. It often means He is working behind the scenes, preparing us for the answers or growing our faith in the waiting. God promises to hear us, and His timing is always perfect.

I also want to add a challenge for you today. Are you taking time to listen? The Holy Spirit is constantly speaking, or guiding us. A conversation is a two way street. Are you constantly talking in your conversation with God, or are you taking time to listen? God speaks to us in many ways - it may be a vision, a voice, a feeling, our intuition, or someone else's word or timing in our life. Pay attention.

1 John 5:14-15 says, "This is the confidence we have in approaching God: that if we ask anything according to His will, He hears us. And if we know that He hears us—whatever we ask—we know that we have what we asked of Him."

Declare out loud:
God hears every word and prayer I speak, even when I feel He is silent. I trust that He listens and responds in His perfect timing. I am confident that my prayers matter to Him. Thank you Lord for hearing my every prayer.

Prayer:
Heavenly Father, I release the lie that You do not hear my prayers. I know that You are a loving and attentive God who listens to every cry of my heart. Help me to trust in Your timing and know that even in silence, You are near. Strengthen my faith as I wait for Your response, and let me never doubt Your love and attention to my needs. I receive the truth that You are always listening. In Jesus' name, Amen.

REFLECT & JOURNAL

"The righteous cry out, and the Lord hears them; He delivers them from all their troubles" (Psalm 34:17).

"Then you will call on Me and come and pray to Me, and I will listen to you" (Jeremiah 29:12).

"But God has surely listened and has heard my prayer" (Psalm 66:19).

Have you been feeling unheard by God? Write out your heart's cry today. Document your prayer so you can come back and see its answer at the end of these 40 days.

_____

_____

_____

_____

_____

_____

_____

_____

_____

_____

_____

_____

_____

_____

DAY 20: PRESENCE
THE LIE: "MY PRESENCE DOESN'T MATTER"

Today, let's confront the lie that says, "Nothing I do really matters." This thought can pull us into a downward spiral, dimming our spirit and hope. But the truth is powerful: our very presence can carry the light of transformation! Think of Peter, who God used to heal others simply by his shadow passing over them. Just like him, you hold the potential to impact the world in ways you may not even realize. Let's dive into the truth that your life and actions make a profound difference.

"As a result, people brought the sick into the streets and laid them on beds and mats so that at least Peter's shadow might fall on some of them as he passed by" (Acts 5:15). Your presence matters. Just as Peter's shadow brought healing to those who were suffering, your life is a beacon of hope and light. You may not see the immediate impact of your actions, but trust that God is using you in ways you may not fully understand. Each kind word, every act of service, and your willingness to love makes a significant difference in this world.

Prayer:
Heavenly Father, I come before You today with a heart full of gratitude for the divine presence You have placed within me. I release any feelings of doubt or insignificance that have overshadowed the truth that I carry transforming power through Your Spirit. Help me recognize the impact of my presence and actions. May my life be a reflection of Your light, bringing healing and hope to those around me. In Jesus' name I pray, Amen.

Declare out loud:
I decree that, just as Peter's shadow brought healing, my presence carries the anointing and healing power of the Holy Spirit. I am a light in the world, shining brightly with the love and truth of Christ, dispelling darkness wherever I go. Through Christ, I am a fragrance of life, spreading the aroma of God's goodness, love, and grace. I declare that my presence is a conduit for supernatural breakthroughs, shifting atmospheres from despair to hope, from sickness to healing. I decree that, as a carrier of God's presence, I bring about divine encounters and open doors for God's glory to manifest.

REFLECT & JOURNAL

Take a moment to recognize the profound impact your presence can have on the lives of those around you. You are a carrier of God's transformative power, and wherever you go, you bring the fragrance of Christ.

"You are the light of the world. A town built on a hill cannot be hidden. Neither do people light a lamp and put it under a bowl. Instead, they put it on its stand, and it gives light to everyone in the house" (Matthew 5:14-16).

Walk in the confidence that your presence is a catalyst for change, shifting the atmosphere and releasing the love and grace of our Savior. Journal about anything that struck you or motivated you today.

_____

_____

_____

_____

_____

_____

_____

_____

_____

_____

_____

_____

_____

DAY 21: PERFECTIONISM
THE LIE: "I NEED TO HAVE IT ALL TOGETHER"

Do you try (ahem *attempt*) to manage every aspect of your life perfectly? The pressure to "have it all together" leaves me feeling inadequate and unworthy, making it easy to believe your worth depends on how well you juggle life's demands. But here's the truth: God does not require perfection. You are loved, chosen, and approved just as you are. Jesus has already chosen you, knowing your imperfections. Your identity is sealed in His love, and salvation is a gift, not something to be earned.

In Luke 10, we find the story of two sisters, Mary and Martha. When Jesus visited their home, Martha was busy trying to manage everything, ensuring that everything was perfect. She was "distracted by all the preparations that had to be made." Meanwhile, Mary chose to sit at Jesus' feet, listening to His teaching. Frustrated, Martha asked Jesus to tell Mary to help her. But Jesus gently corrected her, saying, "Martha, Martha, you are worried and upset about many things, but few things are needed—or indeed only one. Mary has chosen what is better, and it will not be taken away from her" (Luke 10:41-42). This story reminds us that our worth does not come from doing everything right or managing all the details. God values our relationship with Him more than our ability to control every aspect of our lives.

Prayer:
Heavenly Father, I come to You acknowledging that I don't have it all together. I release the lie that I need to be perfect to be loved by You. Thank You for choosing me just as I am. Help me rest in the truth that I am loved, chosen, and approved by You. Thank You for the gift of salvation that I cannot earn but receive freely. In Jesus' name, Amen.

Declare out loud:
I release the lie that I need to have it all together and embrace the truth that I am chosen by God, loved, and accepted just as I am. I am approved by God, not for what I do, but for who I am in Christ. I walk confidently, knowing that God's grace is sufficient for me. I decree that I am chosen by God, set apart, and called for a purpose. I do not need to strive for perfection to be loved or valued. I am already accepted and approved by my Heavenly Father, and I live in the freedom of His grace.

REFLECT & JOURNAL

Reflect on the areas of your life where you feel pressured to "have it all together." Consider why you believe you need to meet certain standards to be accepted. Release those thoughts to God and embrace the truth that He has already chosen you. You don't need to earn His love or prove your worth; it is a gift. Rest in the knowledge that your identity is secure in Him, and you are loved just as you are.

Ephesians 1:4 says, "For He chose us in Him before the creation of the world to be holy and blameless in His sight." You are chosen by God, not based on your performance but on His grace. Ephesians 2:8-9 reminds us, "For it is by grace you have been saved, through faith—and this is not from yourselves, it is the gift of God—not by works, so that no one can boast." Your salvation is a gift from God, already received by His grace.

God's love is unconditional, and you don't have to carry the burden of perfection. Let go of the need to have it all together and embrace the truth that you are already loved, chosen, and approved by the One who knows you fully. Journal what you are releasing to God today that you have been trying to control or make perfect on your own.

_____

_____

_____

_____

_____

_____

_____

_____

_____

_____

DAY 22: HAPPINESS

THE LIE: "I DON'T DESERVE HAPPINESS"

Have you ever felt that happiness is just beyond your reach, as though you don't quite deserve it? The truth is, those feelings of unworthiness can rob you of the abundant life God deeply desires for you. God wants you to experience joy and peace, not because of anything you've done or haven't done, but simply because you are His. Your past mistakes, failures, or regrets don't define your worthiness for happiness. Jesus came to give life abundantly (John 10:10), and that includes deep, lasting joy, freely given because you are His beloved.

Consider the story of Elijah in 1 Kings 19. After an incredible victory over the prophets of Baal, Elijah fell into a dark despair, fleeing into the wilderness and feeling utterly unworthy and defeated. He felt as though his efforts had amounted to nothing, as if he didn't deserve peace or rest. But God met Elijah right there in his brokenness, providing him with food, rest, and gentle encouragement, and reminding him of the purpose and joy still ahead.

God's presence restored Elijah, showing him that he was worthy of love, peace, and purpose, despite his feelings of inadequacy.

Psalm 37:4 states, "Take delight in the LORD, and He will give you the desires of your heart." When you seek your joy in God, He fills your heart with fulfillment. John 10:10 reminds us that Jesus came so we may have life to the full, emphasizing God's desire for you to live joyfully.

Prayer:
Heavenly Father, I release the lie that happiness and joy are beyond my reach or that I'm unworthy of them. Help me to see myself as You see me—loved, chosen, and worthy of every good thing You offer. Heal any part of me that feels unworthy or resistant to joy. Thank You for the abundant life You came to give, full of peace and deep happiness. I open my heart to receive Your joy, and I declare that I am worthy of a life fulfilled by Your love. In Jesus' name, Amen.

REFLECT & JOURNAL

Declare out loud:
I release the lie that I do not deserve happiness and affirm that I am worthy of joy, peace, and fulfillment as a child of God. I choose to walk in the abundant life that Jesus promised me, finding joy in the Lord who fills my heart with gladness. I am loved, chosen, and valued beyond measure.

Reflect on the areas where you've felt unworthy of happiness. Ask God to reveal the lies you've believed about your worth and ability to experience joy. Replace those lies with the truth of who you are in Him: loved, chosen, and worthy of every blessing. Remember that happiness is a gift from your Heavenly Father, freely given to those who love Him.

Proverbs 16:3 encourages us to commit our plans to the Lord, assuring us that He will guide us to success and fulfillment.

Journal today where you can shift your thoughts to gratitude.

_____

_____

_____

_____

_____

_____

_____

_____

_____

_____

DAY 23: FORGIVING OTHERS

THE LIE: "I CANNOT FORGIVE THEM"

Forgiveness is one of God's greatest gifts, yet it can be incredibly difficult, especially after experiencing deep pain or betrayal. Having walked through the darkness of abuse and betrayal myself, I understand how impossible forgiveness can feel. Yet, amidst the pain, I've discovered the incredible freedom that comes with choosing to forgive.

Forgiveness does not condone the actions of those who hurt us. It is a conscious choice to release the invisible chains that weigh us down, often tied to unresolved pain or deep emotional scars. When we choose to forgive, we set ourselves free.

God calls us to forgive because He knows the healing that comes from it. In Matthew 6:14-15, He teaches us that He forgives us as we forgive others. Holding onto unforgiveness not only keeps us bound but also blocks the blessings that He desires to pour into our lives. Today, I want to encourage you to take that courageous step toward forgiveness.

Ephesians 4:31-32 states, "Get rid of all bitterness, rage and anger, brawling and slander, along with every form of malice. Be kind and compassionate to one another, forgiving each other, just as in Christ God forgave you." This verse is a powerful reminder that God asks us to let go of bitterness and embrace kindness and compassion. Forgiveness is a choice, not a feeling, and it's a choice that brings about deep healing and transformation in our hearts.

Prayer:
Heavenly Father, I come before You today, acknowledging that I struggle with forgiveness. I choose to forgive (name the person). Show me, Lord, if there are others I need to forgive—whether it's a parent, spouse, friend, or even myself. I release them to You, Jesus. You are the Judge, and I trust You to handle their actions. I bless them in Your name. Cleanse my heart from any unforgiveness and fill me and my family with Your goodness and healing. Thank You for forgiving me as I forgive others. In Jesus' name, Amen.

REFLECT & JOURNAL

Declare out loud:

I choose to forgive. I release those who have hurt or offended me, freeing them and freeing myself. As I forgive, I am forgiven. I am loved, and peace fills my heart. I walk forward unburdened, open to the fullness of God's grace and joy.

Remember that forgiveness is the doorway to freedom. It doesn't change what happened, but it changes you. It releases the hold of bitterness and opens the floodgates of God's healing in your life. As you let go of past hurts, fill yourself with the love of the Holy Spirit. You are not an empty vessel; you are filled with His goodness, peace, and love.

If you are seeking a deeper prayer to cleanse your bloodline from unforgiveness, I have written one in the back of this book. Forgiveness truly brings freedom, and opens the door to your healing.

Pause and take a breath. Visualize the chains of unforgiveness falling away—this is a significant breakthrough. If forgiveness has been a struggle, be patient with yourself as you heal.

Reflect on areas where forgiveness has been difficult. Who do you need to release?

_____

_____

_____

_____

_____

_____

_____

DAY 24: HEALING

THE LIE: "GOD DOESN'T WANT ME HEALED"

One of the most beautiful promises that God desires is our wholeness. Not just spiritually but physically. God wants you healed. Jesus took your sickness and pain on the cross so you could walk in health and freedom. Every part of your body was designed to function as God intended, and by His stripes, you are healed.

We aren't always certain what could be blocking our healing, (often we need to repent or forgive) or the timing God has for our healing. We learn much in the valleys. Our God is all knowing, so sitting in a space of pain or inner heartache can truly be so crummy. Keep the faith, seek counsel and prayer and cling to the truths spoken on these pages. The enemy comes to steal, kill, and destroy. So let's muster up a mustard seed of faith today to move mountains. Today is a new day, and a great day for miracles.

God's heart is for your healing. Just as Jesus healed those who came to Him, He still desires healing for you today. Speak life over your body, reject negativity, and trust that God's will is for you to be whole.

Prayer:
Lord, I thank You for the healing that comes through Your Son, Jesus. Today, I speak life, health and vitality over my body. I declare that every organ, muscle, and cell operates according to Your perfect design. Forgive me for the times I've spoken negatively about my body, age, or health. I release those words and receive Your healing power, asking in Jesus' Name. I trust that You desire wholeness for me, and I choose to walk in the health You have already provided. Amen.

Declare out loud;
I decree that by the stripes of Jesus, I am healed. I declare that my body, from the cellular level, functions in perfect alignment with God's will. I speak life, health, and strength over myself, rejecting any negative words spoken against my health. I choose to listen carefully to the Lord and walk in His healing promises. I am confident in God's desire to heal me, and I thank Him for restoring me to full health.

REFLECT & JOURNAL

1 Peter 2:24 says, "He himself bore our sins in his body on the cross, so that we might die to sins and live for righteousness; by His wounds you have been healed." Jesus carried our sins and sickness, ensuring that healing is part of the redemption we have through Him. His sacrifice not only brings salvation but healing to our bodies.

James 5:14 reads, "Is anyone among you sick? Let them call the elders of the church to pray over them and anoint them with oil in the name of the Lord." I highly suggest reaching out to elders or a local healing room.

God desires your healing. Journal your thoughts and how you're feeling right now and the healing you are contending for.

_____

_____

_____

_____

_____

_____

_____

_____

_____

_____

_____

_____

_____

DAY 25: PAST

THE LIE: "MY PAST DEFINES ME"

It's incredibly freeing to realize that your past does not define who you are. God is shaping you based on who He's calling you to be, not who you once were. Through the cross, every sin—past, present, and future—is erased by Jesus' blood. His grace is rewriting your story right now.

Consider the story of Paul in Acts 9. Once known as Saul, a man with a reputation for persecuting Christians, he encountered Jesus and was completely transformed. Saul became Paul, one of the most influential apostles and author of much of the New Testament. His past didn't define him; instead, it showcased God's incredible power to redeem and renew.

Paul reminds us of this truth in 2 Corinthians 5:17: "Therefore, if anyone is in Christ, the new creation has come: The old has gone, the new is here!" This verse declares that through Christ, we're not tied to our past. Paul's transformation is proof that with God, even our darkest moments can be redeemed into something beautiful.

Like Paul, we're made new in Christ. Our past no longer dictates our identity. Let go of what's behind you, embrace God's grace, and step boldly into the life He has planned for you!

Prayer:
Thank You God for making a way in the wilderness of my past and bringing forth streams of hope and renewal into areas I once thought were dry. I receive Your forgiveness and extend that grace to myself. Today, I release guilt, shame, and regret, putting on the new identity You have crafted for me through Christ. Thank You for redeeming me and giving me a future filled with hope. Amen.

Declare out loud:
I am redeemed by the blood of Jesus, and my past no longer holds power over me. I am forgiven and free from guilt and shame. I am a new creation in Christ; the old has passed away, and all things have become new. My future is full of hope, purpose, and promise, according to God's plan. I am no longer defined by my past mistakes, but by who God says I am—His beloved and chosen one.

REFLECT & JOURNAL

Your past is not your identity; it is simply a chapter in the story of how God is working for you. Let go of the weight of past mistakes and embrace the new thing God is doing in your life. He has already made a way for you— step confidently into His promises.

"Forget the former things; do not dwell on the past. See, I am doing a new thing! Now it springs up; do you not perceive it? I am making a way in the wilderness and streams in the wasteland" (Isaiah (43:18-19). God calls us to let go of what lies behind and trust that He is creating something new, even in places where we feel barren or lost.

Journal what you're letting go of from your past today, and step forward with the crown before you—as a royal, forgiven child of God.

_____

_____

_____

_____

_____

_____

_____

_____

_____

_____

_____

_____

_____

DAY 26: TRUST

THE LIE: "I CANNOT TRUST ANYONE"

Past hurts, betrayals, or disappointments can cause us to build walls around our hearts. It's understandable, but while people may fail us, our God never will.

Trusting others, especially after experiencing pain, can feel daunting. However, we can draw strength from God's Word. He calls us to trust Him wholeheartedly, even when it feels unsafe. Trusting God with our hearts helps us navigate relationships with wisdom and discernment, allowing us to open up to the right people.

Jesus was surrounded by friends and betrayers, yet He trusted His Father's plan (John 13:21). Similarly, Joseph faced deep betrayal from his brothers, yet chose to trust God's purpose. In the end, Joseph was elevated and able to save his family. His story shows that even when others fail us, God's plan is still good (Genesis 50:20).

Joseph's story teaches us to release the lie that we cannot trust anyone and place our ultimate trust in God, who never abandons His plans for us. Like Joseph, we can trust in God's faithfulness and find the strength to trust again.

Declare out loud:
I declare that I am learning to trust again, starting with trusting God's heart and His plans for me. I reject the lie that I am alone in my struggles and that I cannot trust others. I embrace the truth that, while humans are imperfect, God is always trustworthy and good.

Prayer:
Heavenly Father, I come to You with my fears about trust. Help me to release the pain and disappointment that have led me to believe that I cannot trust others. Teach me to rely on Your faithfulness and to see others through Your eyes. Give me the strength to build healthy relationships and to discern who I can trust. Thank You for Your unwavering love and for being my refuge in times of trouble. In Jesus' name, Amen.

REFLECT & JOURNAL

"Trust in the LORD with all your heart and lean not on your own understanding; in all your ways submit to him, and he will make your paths straight" (Proverbs 3:5-6).

Consider the relationships in your life. Are there individuals you feel hesitant to trust? How can you begin to open your heart to them while keeping your trust anchored in God? Take a moment to journal about a time when trust led to a positive outcome, and ask God to guide you in rebuilding trust where it's been broken.

"The LORD is good, a refuge in times of trouble. He cares for those who trust in him" (Nahum 1:7).

_____

_____

_____

_____

_____

_____

_____

_____

_____

_____

_____

_____

_____

_____

DAY 27: FAITH

THE LIE: "IF I'M STRUGGLING, MY FAITH IS WEAK"

"For we live by faith, not by sight" (2 Corinthians 5:7).

Struggling does not equal weakness; it often reveals our deep yearning for God. Even the most faithful among us experience moments of doubt, fear, and uncertainty. The disciples, despite their closeness to Jesus, faced storms that shook their faith (Mark 4:40). Yet, it was in those moments of struggle that they learned to rely on His power rather than their own.

When Jesus walked on water toward the disciples, they were terrified, thinking He was a ghost. Jesus reassured them, saying, "Take courage! It is I. Don't be afraid." Peter asked to join Him, and Jesus invited him. Peter stepped out, but as he took his eye off Jesus, he grew afraid and began to sink, crying, "Lord, save me!" Jesus caught him and said, "You of little faith, why did you doubt?"

This story illustrates that even when we take steps of faith, fear and doubt can arise. Jesus' response reminds us that struggling with faith does not equate to weakness; instead, it's an opportunity to rely on His grace and power. When life's storms overwhelm us, we can find comfort in knowing that God's grace is sufficient and His strength is made perfect in our weakness.

Declare out loud:
I declare that my struggles do not define my faith; they reveal my dependence on God. I am learning to trust Him more deeply through my challenges. I reject the notion that I am weak when I struggle; instead, I embrace the truth that His grace is sufficient for me.

Prayer:
Heavenly Father, I come before You today, acknowledging my struggles and the feelings of inadequacy that sometimes accompany them. Help me to release the lie that my faith is weak when I face challenges. Teach me to see my struggles as opportunities to rely on Your strength and grace. I am grateful for Your promise that Your power is made perfect in my weakness. Thank You for loving me through every season of my life. In Jesus' name, Amen.

REFLECT & JOURNAL

"And He said to them, 'Why are you afraid? Have you still no faith?'"
(Mark 4:40)
"But he said to me, 'My grace is sufficient for you, for my power is made perfect in weakness'" (2 Corinthians 12:9).

How can you shift your perspective on struggles and see them as opportunities for growth in your faith? Take time today to journal about a recent struggle you faced and how you can lean into God's grace during such moments. Consider what you can learn from your struggles and how they might be drawing you closer to Him.

_____

_____

_____

_____

_____

_____

_____

_____

_____

_____

_____

_____

_____

DAY 28: PEOPLE PLEASING

THE LIE: "I HAVE A HARD TIME PLEASING PEOPLE INSTEAD OF GOD"

"Am I now trying to win the approval of human beings, or of God? Or am I trying to please people? If I were still trying to please people, I would not be a servant of Christ" (Galatians 1:10).

It's easy to get caught up in the need to please others—whether through social media likes, compliments from coworkers, or approval from friends. We often think our value depends on what others think, but that's a lie. Your worth is rooted in God's unchanging love, not human approval. The desire to please people usually stems from insecurity, but in Christ, you are fully loved, accepted, and secure.

King Saul is a powerful example. In 1 Samuel 15, he disobeyed God's instructions because he feared the people and wanted to please them, which ultimately led to his downfall as king.

While seeking human approval can feel overwhelming, you're not alone in this journey. The Holy Spirit, who dwells within you, is your helper and guide, empowering you to discern God's voice above all others. Romans 8:14 says, "For those who are led by the Spirit of God are the children of God." He strengthens you when tempted to seek validation from others and reminds you of your true identity in Christ.

Do you find yourself caught in people-pleasing cycles or feeling that your worth depends on others' opinions? Today, let's break the lie that human validation defines us—God's approval is all we need.

Prayer:
Heavenly Father, I release the lie that my worth is based on other people's opinions. Forgive me for the times I have sought human approval over Yours. Holy Spirit, guide me as I refocus my heart to seek Your validation and live in the truth that I am fearfully and wonderfully made. Help me break free from the trap of people-pleasing and empower me to stand firm in the knowledge that I am fully loved and accepted by You. Teach me to listen for Your voice above all others. In Jesus' name, Amen.

REFLECT & JOURNAL

Declare out loud:

I decree that my worth is not determined by the opinions of others but by God's eternal love for me. I no longer seek validation from the world but find my security in God's unchanging love. I seek to please God above all else, walking in His purpose for my life. I am free from the need for human approval and rest in the security of God's approval.

Reflect on areas where you've sought others' approval and imagine God's voice saying, "You are My beloved, in whom I am well pleased." Release the need for outside validation and embrace the truth that you are fully accepted by Him. Journal today, asking God what you might be seeking from others that He longs to provide for you. Let the Holy Spirit guide you to live for His approval alone, resting in the truth that your worth is secure in Him.

"Fear of man will prove to be a snare, but whoever trusts in the Lord is kept safe" (Proverbs 29:25).

_____

_____

_____

_____

_____

_____

_____

_____

_____

_____

_____

DAY 29: CHANGE

THE LIE: "CHANGE IS TOO HARD"

"Therefore, if anyone is in Christ, the new creation has come: The old has gone, the new is here!" (2 Corinthians 5:17)

"I can do all this through him who gives me strength" (Philippians 4:13).

Today, let's address the belief that "change is too hard." When we're faced with stubborn habits, insecurities, or painful memories, the idea of change can feel overwhelming. But remember, transformation isn't something we do on our own—it's the work of Christ in us.

Think about Peter in the New Testament. Once impulsive and fearful, Peter denied Jesus three times out of fear, yet he went on to become a bold leader in the early church. Through God's grace, Peter was transformed, not by his own strength, but by the power of the Holy Spirit within him. Just as Peter found courage through Christ, we, too, are empowered to step into lasting change.

God's Word assures us that we are being transformed into His image, one step at a time. Just as a caterpillar undergoes a beautiful metamorphosis, we too are being reshaped and renewed in Christ. This transformation may require effort and perseverance, but we are not alone in this process.

Declare out loud:
I declare that I am not limited by my past, for I am a new creation in Christ. I reject the lie that change is hard. I embrace the truth that I am continually being transformed into His image, and with God's strength, I can face any challenge that comes my way.

Prayer:
Heavenly Father, I thank You for the promise of transformation in my life. I release the lie that change is hard and surrender my doubts and fears to You. Help me to embrace the work of the Holy Spirit within me, guiding me toward the changes You desire for my life. Teach me to trust in Your strength as I journey toward becoming more like You. Thank You for Your unwavering love and grace. In Jesus' name, Amen.

REFLECT & JOURNAL

Change isn't about perfection; it's about progress. Each day is filled with opportunities to grow and learn, allowing us to move closer to the person God created us to be. When we declare our commitment to change and rely on His strength, we can navigate the challenges that come our way with grace and determination.

Reflect on the areas of your life where you feel change is challenging. Write down any thoughts or feelings associated with this struggle. Now, consider one small step you can take today toward embracing change. Remember, transformation is a journey, and with God, all things are possible. Take a moment to lay down what feels unchangeable at the foot of the cross. Trust that your Healer and healing are for you today.

"And we all, who with unveiled faces contemplate the Lord's glory, are being transformed into his image with ever-increasing glory, which comes from the Lord, who is the Spirit" (2 Corinthians 3:18).

_____

_____

_____

_____

_____

_____

_____

_____

_____

_____

DAY 30: AWE OF GOD
DEVOTIONAL: HOLY FEAR, REVERENCE, AND AWE OF GOD

Let's pause and take in the majesty and power of the God we serve. The Creator of the universe—the One who spoke stars into existence and carved the depths of the seas—is the same God who calls us His beloved. Sometimes, we can grow so comfortable in His grace that we lose sight of His holiness. Yes, God is love, but He is also sovereign, mighty, and just, deserving our deepest reverence and awe.

This "fear of the Lord" isn't about feeling afraid; it's about recognizing His greatness, humbling ourselves before His power, and honoring His holiness. Proverbs 9:10 reminds us, "The fear of the Lord is the beginning of wisdom, and knowledge of the Holy One is understanding." This reverent fear aligns our hearts with His, guiding us with wisdom and humility.

I remember a season when I was trying to manage everything on my own —work, relationships, my identity. In all my striving, I'd lost sight of God's majesty. When I returned to a place of holy fear, humbly acknowledging His power over my own, I found peace and clarity. That shift put everything in perspective, filling my life with true wisdom.

Today, do you hold a healthy fear of the Lord? Are there areas where you've placed your desires or approval of others above God? Let's return to a reverence for our Creator, letting His greatness guide how we live and love.

Declare out loud:
I decree that I walk in holy fear and reverence of God. I declare that I honor His greatness and sovereignty above all else. I release the desire to control my life and place my trust fully in God's hands. I seek to please Him and live in awe of His power and majesty. I embrace the wisdom that comes from fearing the Lord and humbly walk in His ways. My life is a reflection of His holiness and grace, and I stand in awe of His unfailing love and unmatched power.

REFLECT & JOURNAL

"Let all the earth fear the Lord; let all the inhabitants of the world stand in awe of Him" (Psalm 33:8).

Other Scriptures for reflection: Ecclesiastes 12:13 and Hebrews 12:28-29

Prayer:
Father, I come before You in awe of who You are. I release the lie that I need to be in control, and I receive the truth that You are sovereign, holy, and mighty. Forgive me for the times I've lost sight of Your greatness and taken Your grace for granted. Lord, give me a heart that stands in reverence before You, always acknowledging Your power and Your authority. Lead me in wisdom as I surrender to You in holy fear. Help me to walk in humility, seeking to please You in all that I do. In Jesus' name, Amen.

Where in your life do you need to humble yourself before Him and acknowledge His sovereignty? Write down any areas where you've tried to take control or have lost sight of God's greatness. Now, imagine yourself standing before His throne, overwhelmed by His love and holiness. What does it look like to fully surrender to Him, trusting in His wisdom and power? Journal your thoughts and allow His Spirit to guide you into deeper reverence and awe of who He is.

_____

_____

_____

_____

_____

_____

_____

_____

DAY 31: FAILURE

THE LIE: "I'LL ALWAYS BE A FAILURE"

We've all experienced those gut-wrenching moments when failure—or even sin—seems like a permanent label we can't shake off. But let's set the record straight: failure does not define you; God does!

You are crafted with divine purpose, and His unwavering love is not contingent on your successes or failures. His grace obliterates the notion of failure!

Consider Moses once again, who in a moment of anger killed an Egyptian and fled into the wilderness, fearing he had ruined any chance to fulfill his calling (Exodus 2:11-15). For years, he lived as a shepherd in exile, but God hadn't given up on him. Instead, God called Moses back with a purpose—to lead His people out of slavery in Egypt. What Moses thought was a permanent failure became a stepping stone for one of the most remarkable redemptive journeys in history.

In 1 Samuel 15:22-23, we discover that God prioritizes obedience over mere sacrifice. He is on your side, not against you! Like a loving parent, He desires the best for you and skillfully uses every experience—including failure—to mold His incredible plans for your life.

Prayer:
Heavenly Father, I release the lie that failure defines me. I surrender my shortcomings to You and seek Your forgiveness. Empower me to walk in obedience, even when I stumble. Help me to view every failure as a stepping stone for growth, not a label of my identity. I embrace Your truth today: I am loved, forgiven, and called for Your divine purpose. In Jesus' name, Amen.

Declare out loud:
Failure is NOT my identity; I am defined by God's unwavering love and purpose! I am a child of God, empowered to walk in grace and obedience. I refuse to be defeated by failure—I will be shaped by it for God's glory! I declare that I am chosen and equipped for the good work God has set before me!

REFLECT & JOURNAL

Just as Peter's failure wasn't the end of his story, your failures don't define you either. God's grace is far greater than your mistakes. He uses them to bring you closer to Him and to shape you for His purpose. Walk in the truth that failure is never final in the hands of a loving God.

"But even more blessed are all who hear the word of God and put it into practice" (Luke 11:28).

"Through your offspring all nations on earth will be blessed, because you have obeyed me" (Genesis 22:18).

God's word makes it clear: blessings come from obedience, not perfection. Failure doesn't cancel God's plans for your life. Journal about a failure you will choose to release today.

_____

_____

_____

_____

_____

_____

_____

_____

_____

_____

_____

_____

DAY 32: FORGOTTEN

THE LIE: "GOD HAS FORGOTTEN ABOUT ME"

Beloved, have you ever felt like God has forgotten you? It's easy to believe this lie when life feels overwhelming, when prayers seem unanswered, or when we face trials that stretch our faith. But come with me to reflect on the beautiful truth: you are never forgotten by God. You are deeply cared for and valued, far beyond anything else He created.

Consider the story of Hagar in Genesis 16 and 21. After being mistreated by Sarah, Hagar fled into the wilderness, feeling abandoned and alone. But God found her there, calling her by name and reassuring her that He saw her plight. In her despair, Hagar encountered the God who sees her (El Roi), and He promised her that her son would become a great nation. This beautiful encounter reminds us that even in our lowest moments, God is aware of our struggles and cares for us deeply.

Isaiah 49:15 reminds us, "Can a mother forget the baby at her breast and have no compassion on the child she has borne? Though she may forget, I will not forget you!" Matthew 10:31 tells us, "So don't be afraid; you are worth more than many sparrows," and Romans 8:38-39 boldly declares that nothing can separate us from God's love.

Declare out loud:
I declare that I am not forgotten; I am cherished and valued by God. I embrace the truth that God sees me, hears me, and cares for me deeply. I reject the lie that I am overlooked or abandoned, and I affirm that I am always in His thoughts and heart. I hold on to the promise that God's presence is with me, even in the darkest moments.

Prayer:
Heavenly Father, I come before You today, feeling the weight of the lie that I am forgotten. I release that thought and open my heart to receive the truth that I am never alone. Help me to trust in Your unfailing love and to recognize Your presence in my life, even when I can't see it. Thank You for always being there, for knowing my heart, and for never forgetting me. In Jesus' name, Amen.

REFLECT & JOURNAL

In moments when we feel invisible or overlooked, remember that the Creator of the universe knows your name and cherishes you. He sees you in your struggles and joys, and His thoughts are always toward you. The King of Kings has not turned His back on you; He holds you close to His heart.

Take a moment to reflect on the times you felt overlooked or forgotten by God. What thoughts or feelings arise when you consider this lie?

Write down any experiences that contributed to this feeling of abandonment. Now, invite God to remind you of His constant love and presence in your life. How can you embrace the truth that you are never forgotten? Consider journaling about ways to cultivate a deeper awareness of His love and presence each day.

_____

_____

_____

_____

_____

_____

_____

_____

_____

_____

_____

_____

_____

DAY 33: SIN CYCLE

THE LIE: "I'M DESTINED TO REPEAT MY MISTAKES"

"Forget the former things; do not dwell on the past. See, I am doing a new thing! Now it springs up; do you not perceive it? I am making a way in the wilderness and streams in the wasteland" (Isaiah 43:18-19).

Let's tackle a lie that often creeps in: "I'm destined to repeat my mistakes." This thought can be paralyzing, filling us with hopelessness and regret, as though our past defines our future. But God's promise is clear—He is doing something brand new, right now, in our lives. He calls us to leave our past behind and embrace the fresh path He's creating.

Isaiah 43 reminds us not to dwell on what's behind us because God is busy crafting a way forward, even in places that seem barren. Where we see wastelands of past choices or failures, He brings rivers of new hope, fresh opportunities, and restored purpose. His "new thing" isn't just a chance to move forward—it's a complete transformation, a divine reset that opens our eyes to what He's working out, right here and now.

As new creations in Christ (2 Corinthians 5:17), we aren't held back by old patterns or regrets. Through His grace, God can turn every misstep into a foundation for wisdom and strength. And Romans 8:28 assures us that He weaves every detail—mistakes included—into a tapestry of purpose for those who love Him.

Declare out loud:
I declare that I am not defined by my past mistakes. I release the lie that I am destined to repeat them. I embrace the truth that I am a new creation in Christ, and God is working all things together for my good.

Prayer:
Heavenly Father, I come before You today with a heart burdened by the lie that I am destined to repeat my mistakes. I release this thought and ask for Your healing touch to wash over me. Help me to see the new things You are doing in my life. Grant me the wisdom to learn from my past, but not be bound by it. Thank You for Your grace that covers my failures and gives me hope for a brighter future. In Jesus' name, Amen.

REFLECT & JOURNAL

Step confidently into the new things God is unfolding, knowing He has already made a way. Let go of the past, embrace His grace, and walk in the newness He promises.

Consider the mistakes you've made and how they may have shaped your thoughts about yourself. What lessons have you learned from these experiences? Write down one or two specific ways God has brought good from your past struggles. Allow yourself to let go of the weight of those mistakes, knowing that you are on a journey of transformation. How can you embrace the new things God is doing in your life today?

"And we know that in all things God works for the good of those who love Him, who have been called according to His purpose" (Romans 8:28).

_____

_____

_____

_____

_____

_____

_____

_____

_____

_____

_____

_____

_____

DAY 34: GRATITUDE
THE LIE: "IT'S HARD TO BE GRATEFUL"

Gratitude has a remarkable way of transforming our hearts and shifting our perspective. It serves as a beacon of light in life's storms, illuminating God's blessings even when challenges close in around us. When we intentionally turn our focus to God's goodness—especially during trials—gratitude begins to take deep root within us.

James 1:2-4 tells us, "Consider it pure joy, my brothers and sisters, whenever you face trials of many kinds, because you know that the testing of your faith produces perseverance." This passage reminds us that challenges aren't meaningless; they refine us, building strength, patience, and trust in God. Gratitude, even in hardship, can strengthen our faith, helping us view life through the lens of eternity rather than momentary troubles.

An eternal perspective—the understanding that our time on earth is just a glimpse in light of eternity—fuels our gratitude and helps us see beyond present struggles to God's faithfulness. Psalm 100:4 encourages us to "Enter His gates with thanksgiving and His courts with praise; give thanks to Him and praise His name." Through this lens, we can thank God not just for the blessings we see but for the ways He shapes and sustains us.

Reflect on the story of the ten lepers in Luke 17:11-19. As Jesus traveled through Samaria and Galilee, ten men with leprosy called out for healing, and He healed them all. Yet, only one returned to thank Him. This Samaritan leper, aware of the true source of his blessing, fell at Jesus' feet in gratitude. Jesus asked, "Were not all ten cleansed? Where are the other nine?" This story reminds us of the power of acknowledging God's hand in our lives. Like the grateful leper, we're called to see God's goodness in every blessing and return thanks to Him.

As 1 Thessalonians 5:18 tells us, "Give thanks in all circumstances; for this is the will of God in Christ Jesus for you."

"This is the day that the Lord has made; let us rejoice and be glad in it" (Psalm 118:24)

REFLECT & JOURNAL

Prayer:

Father, I come to You with a heart full of gratitude, even when it feels difficult. Help me recognize Your goodness in my life, even in challenges, and to see how You're growing my faith through trials. Thank You for providing, protecting, and shaping me, and for the gifts of family, home, and hope. I am overwhelmed by Your love and forgiveness. Thank You for the mind of Christ and for setting me free. Help me embrace a spirit of gratitude each day, knowing it aligns me with Your will. In Jesus' Name, Amen.

Declare out loud:

I speak life, love and gratitude that fills my heart. I will focus on the blessings in my life and recognize the goodness of God in every circumstance. I choose joy today. Thank You, Lord, for all You have done! Thank you that I can enter Your gates with thanksgiving in my heart.

As you lay your head to rest at night, reflecting on the blessings you are thankful for can set a powerful tone for waking up with a heart full of gratitude. It's a beautiful reminder that gratitude is a mighty force, shaping our perspective and attitude.

Consider the areas in your life where you find it hard to be grateful. What blessings can you identify, even in the midst of challenges? How can you intentionally cultivate a spirit of gratitude? Write down three things you are grateful for today, and notice how this shift in perspective can influence your attitude and outlook.

_____

_____

_____

_____

_____

_____

DAY 35: POWER

THE LIE: "I AM POWERLESS"

Have you ever felt small, like your efforts don't matter or your voice won't be heard? You have been given divine power and authority. You are not powerless; you are a vessel of His strength. When you accepted Jesus as your Lord and Savior, the Holy Spirit came to dwell within you, and with Him, an immeasurable source of power was placed inside you.

Just as Moses stood before the Red Sea, powerless on his own, he had the power of God behind him to part the waters. Your power does not come from your strength—it comes from God, who empowers you to do the impossible.

"Truly I tell you, whatever you bind on earth will be bound in heaven, and whatever you loose on earth will be loosed in heaven. Again, truly I tell you, if two of you agree on earth about anything they ask for, it will be done for them by my Father in Heaven. For where two or three gather in my name, there am I with them" (Matthew 18:18-20)

Prayer:
Heavenly Father, I thank You for filling me with Your Holy Spirit and empowering me with Your divine strength. I release the lie that I am powerless and embrace the truth that through Christ, I am mighty. Forgive me for the times when I've believed I wasn't enough or that my efforts wouldn't matter. I acknowledge that it is Your power, not mine, that brings about change. Strengthen me to walk in the authority You've given me and to boldly declare Your truth over every area of my life. In Jesus' name, Amen.

Declare out loud:
I release the lie that I am powerless. I am filled with the power of the Holy Spirit. I have the authority to bind and loosen in the name of Jesus. God's strength flows through me, making me a mighty vessel for His work. I am empowered by Christ Himself to do great things in His name. I decree that I am not powerless; I am filled with divine power through the Holy Spirit. I bind every lie that says I am weak and release the truth that I am empowered by Christ to walk in authority and purpose, In Jesus mighty name!

REFLECT & JOURNAL

"Being strengthened with all power according to his glorious might so that you may have great endurance and patience" (Colossians 1:11).

"But you will receive power when the Holy Spirit comes on you; and you will be my witnesses in Jerusalem, and in all Judea and Samaria, and to the ends of the earth" (Acts 1:8).

Take a moment to reflect on any areas of your life where you have felt powerless or incapable. Invite God into those areas and ask Him to remind you of the power He has given you. Write down a situation you feel powerless in and then declare God's authority over it, binding any lies and loosing the truth that you are filled with His strength. Remember, you are not alone—God's power resides in you, and you are capable of doing mighty things in His name.

_____

_____

_____

_____

_____

_____

_____

_____

_____

_____

_____

_____

DAY 36: SAFE & SECURE

THE LIE: "I'LL NEVER FEEL SAFE AND SECURE"

In a world filled with uncertainties and dangers, it's easy to feel like safety and security are out of reach. The enemy uses fear and doubt to convince us that we will always be vulnerable. But God has promised that we are secure in Him. When fear creeps in, we can stand firm, knowing that we are wrapped in His love and protected by His power. And remember He has a plan.

Have you believed the lie that you'll never truly be safe or secure? Do you feel like the uncertainties of life are too overwhelming? Today, release "unsafe" and embrace the truth that God is your refuge and fortress. He surrounds you with His peace and protection.

When anxiety or this lie sneaks in, I have to take a step back, look at the big picture of life, and remember that God has a plan for me. Did you hear that? He is for me—just as He is for you! Plus, with an eternal perspective, I'm living forever in His Kingdom. So even death has no sting.

 "Whoever dwells in the shelter of the Most High will rest in the shadow of the Almighty. I will say of the Lord, 'He is my refuge and my fortress, my God, in whom I trust'" (Psalm 91:1-2).

Prayer:
Heavenly Father, I release the lie that I will never feel safe and secure. I declare that You are my refuge and fortress, and I trust in Your power to protect and uphold me. Surround me with Your peace that surpasses all understanding. Help me rest in the shelter of Your love, knowing that I am secure in You. Thank You, Lord, for being my safe place. In Jesus' name, Amen.

Declare out loud:
I decree that I am safe under the shadow of the Almighty, and no harm can come near me. Fear has no place in my life because God is with me, strengthening and upholding me. I am secure in God's love, and His peace guards my heart and mind. I decree that I am protected by the power of the Lord, and I run to His name as my safe haven. I declare that I am upheld by God's righteous right hand, and nothing can shake me from His care.

REFLECT & JOURNAL

Take a moment to consider the areas in your life where you've felt unsafe or insecure. Now, invite God into those spaces and imagine yourself resting in His embrace. Remember to keep declaring the truth until you truly believe it: God is your unshakable fortress, and in Him, you are always safe. Let go of fear, knowing that you are wrapped in the protective love of your Heavenly Father. Walk in peace and confidence today, knowing He is your shield.

What specific fears or insecurities do you want to hand over to God today? Write them down and then counter each one with a truth about God's protection and love. How does resting in His embrace change your perspective on these fears?

"So do not fear, for I am with you; do not be dismayed, for I am your God. I will strengthen you and help you; I will uphold you with my righteous right hand" (Isaiah 41:10).

"The name of the Lord is a fortified tower; the righteous run to it and are safe" (Proverbs 18:10).

_____

_____

_____

_____

_____

_____

_____

_____

_____

_____

_____

DAY 37: MY GIFTINGS

THE LIE: "I DON'T HAVE ANYTHING TO OFFER"

Have you ever felt that you didn't have anything special to contribute or doubted your ability to make an impact? Today, we confront the lie that suggests you are powerless and insignificant. The truth is, through Christ, the possibilities are endless!

Jesus made it clear that the works He performed were just the beginning. He promised in John 14:12, "Very truly I tell you, whoever believes in me will do the works I have been doing, and they will do even greater things than these, because I am going to the Father." This promise is not just for the apostles—it is for you. You are empowered by the same Spirit that raised Jesus from the dead, equipped to bring healing, hope, and transformation wherever you go.

Consider the disciples: they were not extraordinary by worldly standards— fishermen, tax collectors, and everyday individuals. Yet, when Jesus called them, He empowered them to perform miracles and transform lives. Just like them, you are called and empowered by the same Spirit.

It's easy to fall into the trap of believing you don't have anything significant to offer. Maybe you compare yourself to others or struggle to recognize your gifts. But God sees incredible potential within you. You are not powerless; you are filled with the Spirit of the Living God, and there are no limits to what He can do through you. You have incredible giftings yet to step into.

Prayer:
Heavenly Father, I come before You, grateful for the miraculous power You have placed within me through Your Spirit. I release the lie that I have nothing to offer and embrace the truth that I am equipped to do greater works through You. Help me to see myself as a vessel of Your love and power. I surrender my doubts, insecurities, and fears. Use me, Lord, for Your glory. In Jesus' name, Amen.

Declare out loud:
I decree that I am a miracle worker, empowered by the Holy Spirit to do great works in Jesus' name. I declare that through Christ, I have limitless potential to impact lives and bring glory to God. I decree that I carry the authority to heal, restore, and set captives free by the power of the Spirit within me.

REFLECT & JOURNAL

As you walk in faith, remember that the possibilities are endless. God's power within you is limitless. You may not feel capable, but you are called, chosen, and empowered to work miracles. Trust in what God has placed inside you. Step into the fullness of your calling, knowing you have everything you need because Christ Himself is in you. Oh, the possibilities!

"Now to Him who is able to do immeasurably more than all we ask or imagine, according to His power that is at work within us, to Him be glory in the church and in Christ Jesus throughout all generations, for ever and ever! Amen" (Ephesians 3:20-21).

Take a moment to reflect on the gifts and talents you possess. Write down three ways you can use these gifts to impact others positively. Next write down what gifts you want to have. ASK HIM for them! He loves to give gifts! Stepping out into them can create them. How can you step out in faith and trust God to work through you today?

_____

_____

_____

_____

_____

_____

_____

_____

_____

_____

_____

DAY 38: PLAN

THE LIE: "GOD DOESN'T HAVE A PLAN FOR ME"

Have you ever felt like your life lacks meaning? Have you believed the lie that God doesn't have a plan for you? It's time to let go of that lie and embrace the truth that you are here for a reason. God has intentionally created you with a divine purpose and has set you apart to make a difference in this world.

The story of Esther beautifully illustrates that God has a purpose for each of us, even when we feel insignificant. Embracing her purpose, Esther approached the king, risking her life to save her people. Her courage and faith in God's plan led to the deliverance of the Jews, showcasing how one person can make a profound difference.

Just like Esther, you have been placed in your unique situation for a reason. God has a plan for your life, and He has equipped you to fulfill your purpose. Trust that He will guide you, even when the path seems uncertain.

God's purpose for you was crafted with love and intention long before you took your first breath. Every detail of your journey is known and held by Him. Ephesians 2:10 tells us, "For we are God's handiwork, created in Christ Jesus to do good works, which God prepared in advance for us to do." You are not here by accident; God's plan is intricately woven into every fiber of your being.

Reflect on how deeply God knows you and the incredible purpose He has prepared for you. Even when you feel uncertain, know that you are here with a purpose, divinely orchestrated by the One who created you.

Declare out loud:
I am known, chosen, and loved by God, and I step confidently into His purpose for my life.

Prayer:
Lord, thank You for knowing me so deeply and for setting me apart for Your purpose. Help me to trust in Your plans, even when I don't see the full picture. Remind me daily that I am here on purpose, with a divine calling to fulfill. Amen.

REFLECT & JOURNAL

There are days when we might feel lost, unsure of why we're here or what difference our lives could possibly make. The enemy loves to whisper the lie that we have no purpose, that God doesn't have a plan for us. But the truth is, God has always had a plan for your life, and He has created you with a unique purpose that only you can fulfill.

Do you feel like God has forgotten you? Do you struggle to believe that your life has significance in His grand design? Let go of that lie today and stand on the truth that He has a plan just for you, a beautiful, purposeful path laid out from the very beginning.

_____

_____

_____

_____

_____

_____

_____

_____

_____

_____

_____

_____

_____

_____

DAY 39: SPIRIT LED
THE LIE: "I DON'T KNOW HOW TO
BE LED BY THE SPIRIT"

Have you ever questioned if you're truly being led by the Holy Spirit? It's a common struggle, filled with doubt and uncertainty. We often wonder if we're even capable of discerning His guidance or if we're just missing it altogether. Yet, as believers, we carry an incredible truth within us: the Holy Spirit isn't distant or reserved for a select few; He lives within each of us, actively guiding us into all truth. Today, let's lean into this powerful reality. Through Scripture, prayer, and declaration, we'll embrace the confidence that we are fully equipped to recognize and follow the Spirit's leading in every area of our lives.

In Romans 8:14, the Word reminds us, "For those who are led by the Spirit of God are the children of God." This is not just a promise; it's an identity. Our identity as believers. We are designed to be in tune with the Holy Spirit. Jesus reassured us in John 16:13, stating, "But when He, the Spirit of truth, comes, He will guide you into all the truth." Trusting in the Spirit means believing that we are not alone in our journey and that His guidance is always available to us.

Prayer:
Heavenly Father, I come before You, releasing the lie that I don't know how to be led by the Spirit. I thank You for the gift of Your Holy Spirit, who dwells within me and desires to guide my every step. Help me to silence the noise around me and tune in to Your voice. Open my heart to recognize the gentle nudges and whispers of Your Spirit in my life. I embrace the truth that I am Your child, capable of being led by You. In Jesus' name, I pray, Amen.

Declare out loud:
I declare that I am led by the Holy Spirit and recognize His guidance in my daily life. I decree that I have a spirit of discernment, enabling me to hear God's voice clearly. I proclaim that I am sensitive to the Holy Spirit's promptings, and I trust that He will lead me into all truth. I declare that I walk in confidence, knowing that I am a child of God, and His Spirit empowers me to follow His will. I decree that I am not alone; the Holy Spirit is with me, guiding my steps and illuminating my path.

REFLECT & JOURNAL

Take a moment to consider the areas in your life where you seek guidance. Reflect on moments when you felt a nudge from the Holy Spirit. Write about a specific experience where you sensed His guidance—what did that teach you about listening to Him?

As you journal, think about how you can cultivate a deeper awareness of the Spirit's presence in your daily life. What intentional practices can you adopt to seek His guidance in your decisions and become more attuned to His leading?

"So I say, walk by the Spirit, and you will not gratify the desires of the flesh" (Galatians 5:16).

_____

_____

_____

_____

_____

_____

_____

_____

_____

_____

_____

_____

DAY 40: COMMISSIONING
YOUR COMMISSIONING

Today, we are stepping into the truth of our divine commission from God. Many of us may feel unworthy or unprepared to share the Gospel and make an impact in the world. However, the truth is that each of us has been called by Jesus Himself to go and make disciples. In Matthew 28:19-20, Jesus commands us, "Therefore go and make disciples of all nations, baptizing them in the name of the Father and of the Son and of the Holy Spirit, and teaching them to obey everything I have commanded you." This promise assures us that He is with us always, even to the end of the age.

The call to action is not reserved for a select few; it includes you and me. We are empowered by the Holy Spirit to share the love of Christ and to be His hands and feet in a world that desperately needs Him. Remember that your unique gifts, experiences, and story can be powerful tools for reaching others.

Prayer:
Heavenly Father, I come before You today, releasing the lie that I am not worthy, able or commissioned to make a difference. I thank You for the great commission You have given us and for the reminder that I am part of Your mission in the world. Help me to recognize my value and purpose in Your kingdom. Strengthen my faith to step out and share the love of Christ with those around me. I embrace the truth that I am commissioned, and I will trust in Your guidance every step of the way. In Jesus' name I pray, Amen.

Declare out loud:
I declare that I am commissioned by Christ to go and make disciples, and I embrace this calling with courage and conviction. I decree that I am equipped with the Holy Spirit, empowering me to share the Gospel boldly and authentically. I proclaim that my unique gifts and experiences are valuable tools for reaching others with God's love. I declare that fear and doubt have no hold on me, for I am confident in my mission to spread the Good News. I choose to walk in obedience to God's command, trusting that He is with me every step of the way.

REFLECT & JOURNAL

Please know that you are a vital part of God's plan. Every conversation, act of kindness, and moment of service is an opportunity to share the love of Christ. You are not alone; the Holy Spirit empowers you, and Jesus is with you always.

Consider the people in your life who need to hear the message of Christ. Are there specific ways you can reach out to them? Reflect on your unique story and how it can be a testimony of God's love.

Write about how you can embrace your commission in your everyday life. Who has God placed in your path that you can impact? What steps can you take to share His love more intentionally? Reflect on what it means to you to be commissioned by Christ and how you can live out this calling daily.

_____

_____

_____

_____

_____

_____

_____

_____

_____

_____

_____

_____

_____

_____

_____

SALVATION PRAYER

Heavenly Father,

I come to You with a heart that desires to know the truth and find peace. I confess that I've been trying to do life on my own, and I realize now that I need You. I believe that Jesus is the Son of God and that He died on the cross for my sins.

Your Word says in John 3:16, "For God so loved the world that He gave His one and only Son, that whoever believes in Him shall not perish but have eternal life." I believe that promise, and I trust that You love me deeply, so much so that You sent Jesus to take my place.

I confess my sins and turn away from them now, as in 1 John 1:9 "If we confess our sins, He is faithful and just to forgive us our sins and to cleanse us from all unrighteousness." Please forgive me for the things I've done that were against Your will, and cleanse me from the inside out.

Romans 10:9 teaches, "If you declare with your mouth, 'Jesus is Lord,' and believe in your heart that God raised Him from the dead, you will be saved." Today, I declare that Jesus is my Lord and Savior. I believe in my heart that He was raised from the dead, and through this, I receive the gift of salvation.

Thank You for Your grace, Lord. Thank You for the new life You are giving me. 2 Corinthians 5:17 says, "Therefore, if anyone is in Christ, the new creation has come: The old has gone, the new is here!" Today, I step into that new life as a child of God, leaving my old ways behind.

I ask You, Jesus, to come into my heart, lead me, and help me live according to Your will. Teach me to trust You with my whole heart, as Proverbs 3:5-6 says: "Trust in the Lord with all your heart and lean not on your own understanding; in all your ways submit to Him, and He will make your paths straight." I surrender my life to You completely, and I trust that You will guide me in every step.

I thank You, Lord, for saving me, for loving me, and for giving me eternal life. In Jesus' name, Amen.

Be sure to release and then receive in this prayer. When you empty yourself, you must fill back up with Holy Spirit so you aren't an empty vessel for evil to come in.

Dear Jesus,
As a royal priest in Your Kingdom, I come before You today to ask for forgiveness on behalf of my bloodline and my children's bloodlines from ALL generations past—back to Adam. I acknowledge and repent for any sins committed, including bloodshed, idolatry, sexual immorality, witchcraft, false witness, evil hearts, and all that is detestable to You.

I release these burdens and generational curses, renouncing any ties that bind my family to these sins. In Your mighty name, I declare that they have no hold over us.

We receive the precious blood of Jesus to cleanse our bloodline from all iniquities, and we thank You, Jesus, for this cleansing!

Now, we open our hearts to receive Your peace, love, patience, and all the fruits of the Spirit. Fill us to overflowing with Your Holy Spirit, Lord, so that we may not remain empty vessels for evil to enter.

We put on the full armor of God (Ephesians 6) and go forth boldly, knowing we are forgiven, cleansed, and fully loved. Thank you, Jesus, for your grace and mercy that transforms us.

In Your holy name, we pray. Amen.

ABOUT
the author

Suzy Holling is a passionate author, life coach, and photographer dedicated to guiding individuals on their journey toward healing and freedom. With a heart for helping others discover their true selves, she creates transformative experiences that inspire personal growth and empowerment.

Nestled on a serene farm in eastern Washington, Suzy balances her creative pursuits with family life and raising three kids alongside her husband.

In addition to her writing and coaching, Suzy leads in-person retreats for women, providing a safe space to break free from past limitations and embrace their authentic identities. Her retreats are a beautiful blend of connection, reflection, and encouragement, designed to help women rediscover their worth and purpose.

With her warmth and enthusiasm, Suzy invites you to embark on a journey of self-discovery and transformation, reminding you that you are never alone in your quest for healing and wholeness. Visit www.suzyholling.com to learn more about her work and join her on this incredible adventure.

Made in the USA
Las Vegas, NV
30 November 2024